"It is thorough and right on target. Any pa.... ....uy veginning the process of trying to choose a college should have a copy."
—Gregory D. Goldsmith, Associate Director of Admissions,
Cornell University

"Takes a complicated, confusing process and brings sanity and strategy to the college selection process. I recommend it strongly."
—Barbara-Jan Wilson, Dean of Admissions and Financial Aid,
Wesleyan University

"Good reading with lots of excellent advice on how to conduct oneself as a parent during this most difficult year of parenthood. . . . Will go a long way toward relieving the family pressures associated with the process of searching for and being admitted to an appropriate college."—G. Gary Ripple, Ph.D., Director of Admissions,
Lafayette College

"Reduces [an incredibly complex process] to terms that are easily understood and appreciated. The manner in which voices of experience are woven into the presentation is . . . reassuring to the concerned parent."—Peter Van Buskirk, Dean of Admissions,
Franklin & Marshall College

"A superb job of pointing out the challenges that applicants and their families face in college admission and provides straightforward and helpful advice on how parents can smooth the process."
—David L. Gould, Dean of Admisisons, Brandeis University

"Sums up the anxieties of both parents and students, and gives practical advice to overcome them."—Nanette H. Clift, Director
of Recruitment, Washington University in St. Louis

"A comprehensive guide. . . . Should prove helpful and encouraging to parents and their children alike. Its advice is especially respectful of the different roles appropriate to parents and to their children in this very important adventure."—Elizabeth Mitchell, Assistant
Vice President for University Undergraduate Admissions,
Rutgers University

Getting YOUR CHILD *into* COLLEGE

Getting YOUR CHILD *into* COLLEGE

WHAT PARENTS MUST KNOW

....

Susan Newman

with Janet Spencer King

ST. MARTIN'S GRIFFIN ☙ NEW YORK

Design by Sara Stemen

Library of Congress Cataloging-in-Publication Data

Newman, Susan.
    Getting your child into college : what parents must know / Susan
Newman with Janet Spencer King.—1st ed.
        p. cm.
    "A Thomas Dunne book"—T.p. verso.
    Includes bibliographical references.
    ISBN 0-312-14107-6
    1. Universities and colleges—United States—Admission. 2.
Parent and child—United States. 3. College choice—United
States.
    I. King, Janet Spencer. II. Title.
    LB2351.2.N49   1996
    378.1'05—dc20   95-36302
                                                               CIP

A Thomas Dunne Book
First St. Martin's Griffin Edition: February 1996

10 9 8 7 6 5 4 3 2 1

To our soon-to-be college-bound children:

Andrew, Jamie, and Megan

ACKNOWLEDGMENTS
■■■■■■■■■■■■■■■■■■■■■■■■■■■■■■■■■■■■

To many, probably most, parents who embark with their teen on the college search, the journey is full of anxiety and trepidation. Often it becomes filled with friction as well, usually caused by the parents' and children's lack of information about both practical and emotional issues; the timetable is confusing, the responsibilities are fuzzy, and the search seems overwhelming.

We set out to write a book that would clarify the mystery and misconceptions surrounding this life-altering family journey. To do this we went to the source: parents and students who had been there and experts in the field. Families shared their concerns and feelings as well as their solutions, stories, and insights—all of which should serve to guide you and your teen on a course made easier by theirs.

Our experts included the people who are major forces in helping shape and determine your teenager's ultimate college choice: admissions directors, high school guidance counselors, and educational consultants. Their observations and advice about choosing the colleges right for your child, as seen from the inside, should smooth the process of application for you both and give you the confidence that comes from knowing you're doing it right.

Some experts were particularly involved in our research—answering endless questions, giving fully of their time and expertise, leading us to many other helpful professionals, as well as contributing students and parents. Our special thanks to Anne Franzese, director of college guidance in a New Jersey high school; Gwen Cleghorn, a college guidance counselor who spent many years at The Westminster Schools in Atlanta; Geraldine Fryer, an educational consultant in New York and Washington, D.C.; and Barry McCarty, director of student financial aid at Lafayette College.

As you embark on your grand adventure with your teen, our hope is that this book will help you turn this experience into a gratifying one for you and your child. Our best wishes to you both.

Susan Newman
Janet Spencer King

CONTENTS

■■■■■■■■■■■■■■■■■■■■■■■■■■■■■■■■■■■■■■

INTRODUCTION

■■■■■■■■■■■■■■■■■■■■■■■■■■■■■■■■■■■■■

It's one of those parenting experiences that always seemed to lurk somewhere in the future, to be confronted at a later date. But suddenly it's here: Your child is about to start the college-search odyssey. In an ideal world, this would be an efficient, to-the-point process. In the real world, it's generally anything but. For most families the college search is filled with emotional upheaval, coupled with a sense of too much to do—and too little time to do it.

The urgency you feel has some basis in reality. There *is* a lot to be done in a short period of time. First, there is a bewildering array of schools to consider. Then there are other parents, relatives, and your child's peers adding their opinions to the mix you're already dealing with. And there are the specialists—from high school counselors to independent consultants, each one ready to help if you know what to ask. But no one experiences the overwhelmed feelings more than the main character in this drama, who, of course, is your college-bound child.

For both parents and child, the college search has a

multitude of potential rewards in addition to the obvious one of securing a place in a freshman class. The search process is a true opportunity for teenagers to gain and to sharpen many life skills. Students develop some of these skills during their high school years, but others will be new to them. They will have to research areas previously unknown, write letters and essays, be interviewed, and pare down a mammoth mass of information to comprehensible size and scope. They also will need to explore who they are, to gain a greater awareness of themselves, so that they can determine the kinds of learning and lifestyle experiences they want in their future. It's an opportunity, yes, but a challenge as well—one that daunts even the most mature students.

For you, the parent, the rewards are more subtle. Your child is preparing to go off on her own, and that realization is relieving and frightening, joyous and unbearably sad. "Sending my kids to college was wrenching for me," recalls a Delaware mother. "I dreaded their leaving the full year before. When it was actually time for them to go, I went into mourning that lasted for weeks," she reports, still surprised by the depth of emotion she experienced. (However, she also explains that everyone adjusted quickly. "At Thanksgiving, I was thrilled to see them, but," she adds, "I was happy to see them go. We were comfortable getting back to our separate lives.")

In spite of the emotional turmoil, you'll have to keep your head about you, prompting your child at times, piloting only if you have to. Don't assume your own college search those many years ago will be enough to ground you in college reality today. It won't be. In fact, you'll be surprised as you go along how different so much of the search is now. Your image of yourself as a capable parent may be almost as it was in those days after your newborn was placed in your arms. How on earth am I going to handle this? you probably thought then. Now, as then, you are suddenly up against an experience that calls on you to act knowledgeably about something you know little about.

Of course there is a major difference from the challenge you faced as a new parent. That child is—or should be—the major architect in the decisions that will build his future. No longer the leader, you have become the assistant as your child makes life-altering choices. For many parents it isn't an easy position. You probably are incredibly invested in your child's feelings—and future success. Despite all your good intentions, you'll need to be wary of how quickly your investment can turn you into a tyrant. "The whole experience was so frustrating," reports a California dad. "I could see what my son should do and what was best for him in the long run, but he seldom felt the same way. It was unbelievably hard for me, but I finally learned to back off from what were, after all, his decisions. Until that point, he and I were locked in battle."

A PARENT'S PREP COURSE

The college search is a tall order for most parents, but one you *can* handle and well. Consider this book your "prep course," in which you'll learn what emotions your child is probably experiencing and the ones you'll go through. You'll focus on what your role is and what it is not; how to be genuinely helpful and how to transition out when your helpfulness goes overboard. It will guide you each step of the way, from the first glimmerings about possible schools to the day you celebrate admission. Because *Getting Your Child into College* is for parents, the material on the pages that follow comes from your point of view. This guide should bolster your spirits along with your knowledge and give you means to avoid some of the tension and conflict that is often a part of the college-search odyssey. This is a stressful year and experience, but it's possible to turn the process into one that's manageable, even harmonious.

Research for this book comes from extensive interviews with high school counselors, college admissions staffs, independent consultants, and school psychologists. These are the people who introduce and clarify the paper chase that college applications require. They also present truth about the rumors and outright myths that exist concerning getting into college (especially top-level ones). It is with these expert voices that you will turn into a savvy college-search adviser for your child.

You'll hear from other voices as well in this book. They are the parents who have been there, sharing their memories of the pain, the angst, the confusion, and the glory. You are not alone!

The goal of *Getting Your Child into College* is to help you turn the college search into a cooperative adventure for you and your teen. Of course, as on every journey there will be bumps along the way, but overall, and certainly in the end, it can be a happy and satisfying journey for you both.

Chapter One

STUDENTS UNDER FIRE
■■■ ■

"Hello. My name is Ginny and I'm having a nervous breakdown." The young lady making this comment wasn't at an Alcoholics Anonymous meeting or in her therapist's office. She was meeting her high school counselor shortly after she had started the college search. Ginny is one of the hundreds of thousands of high school students in this country who each fall undergo the pressure of searching out and gaining admission into the right college.

A look at the lengthy list of stress factors that gang up on the student applying to college quickly makes it evident why it is such a hard time. It's the rare student who handles this experience with aplomb, and most end up like Ginny, incredibly stressed out. "I don't think there is a single child who goes through the process without stress," reports Anne Franzese, director of college guidance at a northeastern private school.

Even during periods when the search doesn't seem to be in the forefront, for your child the pressure is like an undertow, constantly present and ready to knock him off balance at anytime. "We make so much of college applications," points out educational consultant Geraldine Fryer, in Rye, New York. "We have too many students too close to the edge."

A PRESSURE COOKER ENVIRONMENT

The following stressors typically besiege all kids throughout the turbulent months of the college search. Even though your child may not say much about any or all of these, you can bet they are present to some degree.

•**Fear of failure.** Most students, including those who find academics a breeze, worry that they won't be accepted at the college of their choice—or at any at all. Many spend hours agonizing about the arrival of thin letters that by their very size foretell rejection. Some applicants are so obsessed with possible rejection, they won't apply to the schools they would most like—and have a good chance of getting in— for fear of being turned down. One mother observed: "My daughter's become less confident about her ability to get in. She keeps wondering if she's good enough."

•**Fear of disappointing parents.** Failure has another face, one that is even more painful for some teenagers. "My worst fear is that I will disappoint my parents," a Philadelphia junior says with a sigh. "I worry constantly about it," she admits. Yet a classmate from the same school puts his concern another way: "I know this is a chance to make my parents really proud of me. But that's a pressure in itself. It's become like a drive in me—make Mom and Dad proud."

•**Deadline anxiety.** Deciding on and applying to colleges is a condensed experience, one that for most students and their parents ultimately falls into a period of just a few months. Teens must cram a huge amount of activity into very little time: applications, essays, and SAT or ACT preparation combine with the routine pressure of homework, social life, and, for some teens, a part-time job. This happens at the same time students feel their grades are especially critical. "This semester is my last chance to prove what I can do," says a nervous high school senior.

To compound the grade stress, "Somewhere between the middle of September to the middle of October, kids panic," reports former guidance counselor Betty Van Zandt. "They decide they are behind and that all the other kids are on top of things and know exactly where they want to go." This is seldom the case, but the pressure builds anyway.

•**Unrealistic expectations.** Students who tend to be perfectionists don't reduce their standards one bit during the college search. If anything, they raise them. These teens nag at themselves constantly about the validity of their choices and how they compare to their friends' choices and experiences. They agonize over every blank line on their applications. Without question, they are their own worst taskmasters.

•**Parents' preferences.** When parents have a school in mind for the child, the pressure is on. If the child doesn't want the school, she knows trouble may be ahead. "My mom wanted me to go to Wellesley in the worst way, but I had no intention of being her wish fulfillment. She had always felt bad she hadn't gone there, but really, what does that have to do with me?" asks Heidi, a South Carolina senior. Still, Heidi knows that there will be a show-down about the school. "Mom isn't going to give this one up easily."

When the teen does want the school, anxiety may present itself in a twofold manner. The most obvious is that the teen fears he may not get in. "My family has a long history of going to Dartmouth, but I'm pretty sure my grades aren't going to measure up. I feel like the weak link," says a New Jersey boy. On the other hand, some college-bound teens feel conflicted about "giving in" to the parent's dreams, hating, in teenage fashion, to admit that they may want the same thing as their parents do.

•**Parents' misconceptions.** It's not uncommon for parents to be unclear about their child's true abilities. This can add to the pressure the student is under. The student may know that the prestigious names on her parents' list aren't realistic for her, but the parents may not be able to see it that way. Their fantasy can create havoc for the child's emotional well-being.

•**Peer upheaval.** Quite often, children who have grown up together may find themselves competing for admission to the same school, an awkward position at best. Sometimes friendships crumble. "I watch kids who have been friends for years break up because one got into the coveted school and the other didn't," reports a high school guidance counselor. "In some cases the kids would have worked it out, but the parents got involved. One dad actually accused another father of pulling strings to get his daughter's acceptance. Needless to say, that friendship never recovered."

For the first time too, students may feel intense competition with each other. "I started searching out the weak points in my friends who are applying to the same schools

I am," admits a California senior. "It's unnerving. We all know we're competing with each other, but it's tough to say anything about it."

There is also the pressure of the *unknown* competition to deal with. In some ways it's worse than the competition from fellow students because, as psychiatrist Harvey Ruben points out in his book, *Competing*, people tend to over-estimate unknown competitors' strength. "Every time I think about the valedictorians around the country who are applying to Brown, I feel like I'm going to vomit," says Pamela, a senior in Chicago. "I'm absolutely frantic that their records are going to make me look like I slept my way through high school," she says in spite of an admirable transcript.

•**Life in a fishbowl.** Adding to these complex strains is the very real fact that students are performing the college search in a fishbowl, clearly visible for others to observe. Applying to college is definitely not a private matter. It is the topic of conversation for months, sometimes years, both in and outside of school. Relatives, friends, even neighbors who hardly know the child ask about college preferences and make recommendations. And they follow up to find out the results, including what happened to their recommendations.

Too often, too many people are eager to foist opinions about the "right" school. While this interest is not unkindly motivated, it is highly unsettling to the students who are on center stage, teens who by their very nature prefer a measure of secrecy about their lives. "I had one senior come in just after Christmas break who was a complete mess," recalls a guidance counselor at a large Boston high school. "She had applied to schools that were really appropriate choices for her, but over the holidays her relatives got into what she should do. They absolutely overwhelmed her with their own experiences. It didn't matter that most of them didn't have the foggiest idea about this girl's abilities or interests. The whole thing was terrible for her. Unfortunately, it's not that unusual," the counselor comments.

•**Fear of mistakes.** High school juniors and seniors who haven't thought beyond what to have for lunch find themselves dwelling on their futures—the colleges that will fulfill their fantasies and give them the background and name they need to get ahead in a career. "I'm signing up for a special elective at my school," reports a New York City sophomore at a private school. "It is a program to keep us from making a mistake about the colleges we choose so we can be sure to get good first jobs," she explained to a stunned group of adults at a large party.

Today's students are being fed a constant stream of media reports about recent college graduates who are having difficulty getting jobs and supporting themselves in a reasonable style. High school students have no idea what their own reality will be, and many worry about it. Few students have any real awareness of what they want to do professionally—and they worry about that too. "I know that if I had a specific career in mind I could tailor my college choice around it," explains Marlene, a Washington, D.C., junior. "My biggest worry is selecting the right school, one that will be good for my career. I really don't want to have to transfer," she says.

The college search is stressful because it *is* a major life decision and step toward independence. Consequently there is no way students can avoid all of the stress it entails. However, you can play a key role in helping your child weather this sometimes powerful emotional tempest.

As a parent you will aid your child most by remaining positive, hopeful, and, above all, realistic. "We live in an age of designer children," Carol Perry, Ph.D., director of high school counseling, observes wryly. "Parents don't want their child to be average, but at this stage, especially, they must look at what really matters in life and what is most important to their kids."

Carefully consider what the expectations are that you have of and for your child. Are they truly in line with who your child is? Do they fit with what your child wants for himself? One of the finest things you can do for both of you is to have some heart-to-heart discussions. Listen to what your child is telling you. Sort out the debris of your own inappropriate expectations cluttering the situation and proceed with reality as your premise.

You'll be called on to act with extraordinary tact in this process (see Chapter 5 for a compete discussion of the parent's role), but you'll be invaluable to your child if you are grounded with knowledge. The pages that follow will give you a clear picture of this process generally.

•**Be watchful.** For your student specifically, keep a careful eye on the pressures that surround her—and her reactions to them. If you see a child becoming overwhelmed, help her establish priorities; teens who are doing too much may need reminding of what matters most. Cindy, a Morristown,

New Jersey, junior, was involved in numerous extracurricular activities but decided it would be to her advantage to do more. She joined choir, in addition to band and the swim team. When she began to develop abdominal pain that was intruding on her swimming, she was nearly distraught with worry about what to do. "My mom pointed out to me how overloaded I was making myself. She helped me see that I would end up hurting my efforts and enjoying my life less if I didn't give myself a break." Cindy stopped swimming, something she had done since she was seven. "It was hard at first, but I was so happy to have more time. It ended up being absolutely the right decision for me," she says.

•**Expect the emotional gamut.** A student may have trouble sleeping or show signs of increased restlessness. Another might start nailbiting or other behaviors you've never seen before. "One day the kids are very mature," observes Dr. Perry. "Then the next day they are acting like young children. Parents need to be sensitive to these fluctuations." Be understanding about the strain your child is under and don't make light of it—to the teen the problem is very real.

•**Allow your child to enjoy senior year.** This is a once-in-a-lifetime experience, the chance to be top dog after twelve years of schooling. Of course you'll want to be sure your child is following through on the search, but don't ruin the year with constant harping about applications, test scores, and grades.

•**Bring up potentially sensitive issues.** There aren't any good solutions to such issues as friends vying for the same spots at a university. That's the nature of life. But you can help your child relieve some of the pressure—and perhaps even some guilt she might have about trying to "beat out" her best friend—by talking about it. Acknowledge to your child that these are tough issues that evoke mixed emotions. Talk about them without making judgments, and encourage her to do the same. This will help her realize that stress and the host of other, sometimes difficult feelings are part of the process, that she's normal and so are her feelings.

Chapter Two

PARENTS HAVE FEELINGS TOO
■■■■■■■■■■■■■■■■■■■■■■■■■■■■■■■■■■■■■■■

Whether you actually make the list of schools to which your child applies, or he does it himself, you have been influencing him about college for years, really since the moment of birth. Even in homes where parent-child conversations didn't focus on college per se, kids have a strong fix on parental attitudes and expectations about higher education. "It's just a given in my family," says a graduating senior. "The sky is blue, the sun comes up in the morning, and Katherine's going to college. It's always been that way and I knew it when I was five. At my kindergarten graduation, we had to say what we wanted to be. Some kids said a cab driver, some said an artist. I said a doctor. I guess I knew then that higher learning would play a big role in my life!"

Another student, a young man, recalls it as an early pressure. "Ever since I can remember my parents would say about anything I did, 'Well, then how are you going to get into college?' I knew I couldn't decide college wasn't for me. Not if I wanted to stay in the family," he says with only a hint of a chuckle.

In spite of many families' lifelong emphasis on education, when the time comes to act on finding a college, there is a surprising range of parental attitudes. On one end are parents who are only vaguely aware that their child is filling out applications. In fact, many parents would envy an Atlanta mother who reveals her surprise when her son announced his college plans. "He told us at dinner he was going to Duke. I assumed he was starting his wish list, but no, he really was going to Duke. He had applied for early admissions and been accepted. I had no idea!" That's reminiscent of women in the later stages of pregnancy hearing about another woman's easy-as-pie labor—the way you'd love this experience to be but you can be almost positive it won't.

OFF THE DEEP END

The other end of the scale is undoubtedly where many more parents cluster. This is where the involved, the *anxious* hover. Many parents are so immersed in the process, there's little room left for their child. "My daughter asked me to quit calling her high school counselor so much," admits one mother. "I knew it was ridiculous to be calling two or three times a week, but I almost couldn't help myself." Another mother reached the point that her daughter says, "I hid in my room to avoid my mom's constant nagging at me about the applications. I knew what I had to do and I knew I would get to it. But she was so hyper I really couldn't stand being around her."

While being concerned is reasonable, the hysteria and chronic anxiety many parents go through is neither healthy nor productive. The person who ends up suffering the most

16

in this scenario is usually the student. "My biggest problem," notes independent consultant Geraldine Fryer, "is to get the parents off the student's back. These parents don't listen to what their children are saying. They become fixated on one issue or one school. They don't give their kids credit for what they know about themselves."

Not surprisingly, there are some real anxiety issues at work deep in overinvolved parents' psyches. Here are some fears and hopes that underly parents' meddlesome approaches.

•**College is the sole key to the child's future.** Across dinner party tables and from barbecue to barbecue, you hear the myth that without the right college, a child's future is doomed. New York educational consultant Jane Kolber reports that this mentality starts among parents of prekindergarteners. "Unfortunately, the mind-set begins very early. The parents of these little ones are so afraid if they send their child to the 'wrong' preschool the child will never make it to Harvard. They're so anxious."

Yet another group is fixated on the rank of college and the child's future, but from a different point of view. These are parents who didn't go to college themselves. As lecturer and teacher Alfie Kohn writes in his book *No Contest*, "If our parents never got very far in school, we must not merely take advantage of the chances they never had—we must be the very best. . . ." A more subtle factor at work here, observes Fryer, is that parents who did not attend college themselves often are "intimidated by the process." She adds that some feel guilty. "They think they are unable to help their child in the process, and that simply isn't true. They know their child's strengths and weaknesses as well as any other parent knows her child's."

Overcompensation is sometimes the game plan. Says one high school senior whose mother quit school before college: "My mother is driving me nuts with her pressure about school. She wants me to apply to every school she ever heard of because she is scared I won't get into the schools I choose. Her fear is making me a nervous wreck."

•**The need to protect their child.** Haverford College admissions director Delsie Phillips has been in the business for nineteen years. But it wasn't until she had her own child that she truly understood how invested parents become in their children and so how emotionally wrenching the process could be. "I understood it intellectually before," she says, "but now I understand it emotionally. I can see why parents get so upset at this juncture. It's such a hard time for kids and they worry so much. You want to protect your own from the spills and falls that lie ahead. Most parents know they shouldn't be doing that, but it's such a natural reaction it's hard not to."

One of the most popular methods of rearing kids in the last generation has been through kindness, understanding, and bolstering self-esteem. Then along comes a process that can be utterly ruthless in revealing a child's performance, warts and all. If a child isn't a good tester, parents fear he will be humiliated when his test scores come in lower than those of his friends. A child who has squeaked through his academics for one reason or another will have to pay the piper when his friends gain admission at prestigious schools and he doesn't. "For me it is like being back in the play groups when my son was two or three," explains the mother of a junior in high school. "I could see the hurt feelings that were inflicted at the tot lot, but I could reassure him. I can't do that anymore so I want to take over the search," she admits. This woman's son is highly artistic but not academically oriented the way his friends are, and he finds the differences difficult to accept. "I know I could navigate him into schools that would be right for him and spare him the pain of rejection from the schools his friends want. But he is stubborn and will do it his way, even though I know it's going to be a pretty shaky proposition," she says.

•**Prestige for the family.** For many parents, life is a competition, and they surely don't give up at this point. College acceptance, the decal on the back of the van that commands respect from other drivers, is the culmination of a competition that began when these parents struggled to be sure the child got into the "right" nursery school. "For some parents the college their child attends is an extension of them," explains psychologist Carol Perry. "It's the same thinking that drives buying decisions and keeps expensive cars and fashion houses in business."

A suburban mother itemizes almost with disbelief the schedule of a neighbor boy, the son of intensely competitive parents. "He's bright, not brilliant, but his parents will have none of that," she says. "His parents had him at Berlitz for an evening class to bolster his language course. He had tutors for advanced math where he didn't belong in the first place. Last summer his parents sent him to a camp that tutors campers for the SATs!" This woman calls people like her neighbors "berserkers." These people, she explains, "are flipping out. We went on a tour of the George Washington University campus and some parents were asking about statistics on the graduates, convoluted questions with answers they thought would give them the real lowdown on how their kids would do in life if they graduated from GW. That's just nuts," she concludes.

One boy gave in to his parents' demand that he apply only to the schools they wanted in spite of his guidance counselor's vociferous objections. He ended up without a place in a freshman class—and with a lot of bitterness. "I was sure these were not the right schools for me," he reports. "My parents were so adamant that this was the only way I should go I finally gave in and did it their way. You can't imagine how humiliated I felt when I wasn't accepted. I really resented them too because I *knew* this was how it was going to turn out," he says.

•**Torn between parents**. Some families in which parents are divorced have two ongoing camps: Mom's and Dad's. Caught between the warring parties are the kids. The problem can erupt into fireworks, or the child fears it might, when Dad wants Notre Dame and Mom wants Vassar, for example. "I worry that no matter what I decide, it's going to disappoint one parent or the other," a high school junior complains.

•**Alumni kids: It runs in the family**. The loyalty and devotion many people feel to their own alma mater can be consuming. Parents dress their infants in baby sweatshirts with their school's logo, they keep a decal on their car decades after the fact, football games remain a must, and they still spend countless hours in conversation about their "good old" college life. It goes almost without saying that these parents have plans for the graduating child.

As often as not, teens have different ideas. "When my dad and I went to his school for my interview, he had a great time talking to all the people he knew. They joked about their years together when they were in school and he was laughing and happy. But frankly," says this high school senior, "I knew this could never be my school. It was my dad's and it always would be. I want my own school," he adds resolutely.

Then too, students sometimes misinterpret a parent's continued alumni affiliation with a college or university, and the pressure they put on themselves causes an unproductive rift between parent and child. "I know my dad wants me to go to Georgia, but I won't even apply there," says a high school junior in North Carolina. Her father reveals in a separate conversation that he doesn't care where his daughter goes. "I want her to select the right school for her, but she is putting a lot of energy into worrying about Georgia for my sake."

FINDING THE RIGHT MIND-SET

To some degree, the anxiety and pressure parents go through is understandable. This is true in particular for parents of children who have their heart set on the top-ranked schools in the country. A peek into the admissions office at Harvard is more than sobering for the students and parents who see the Crimson as a dream fulfillment. Applicants from the ranks of the best and brightest, alumni sons and daughters, athletes and those with special talents can swell the numbers any given year to almost 18,000. Acceptance will go to just over 1,600 students, less than 10 percent of the applicants. A similar situation exists at the University of Pennsylvania. In a recent year 15,000 students vied for 2,300 openings.

"The applicants at the loftiest schools are the leaders in their class," observes consultant Jane Kolber. "The kids have taken the AP courses, the toughest honors classes, and received top, top grades. So if your child is a good kid with an A− average and a cluster of activities including, maybe,

Student Council president, does he have a chance of getting into one of these schools? Maybe yes, maybe not," she concludes.

"I feel I have to be competitive because the schools are," says a New Jersey mother defending her aggressive stance. "Maybe that sounds like an excuse, but I think it's simple reality. My daughter doesn't get how much competition she's up against, so I feel I have to compensate."

Most parents will serve their child better—and more effectively—by assuming a lower-key approach. Parents have much more *indirect* influence on a child's college search than they may realize. Just as your unspoken attitudes shaped your child's thinking about education growing up, the way you view the college search also will play a key role. In addition, your attitude may be exactly what she needs to make level-headed, appropriate moves and decisions.

You'll need to clarify your own thinking and emotions to be of real value to your child. First-timers, in particular, do well to find a friend who has been through the process. Other parents experiencing the search at the same time aren't good candidates for this sensitive position. Not only are they dealing with their own questions and pressures, some have their own, private agendas as well. As a mother who came from India and was especially boggled by the demands of college-hunting commented, "I had the distinct impression that the parents at my son's school wanted their kids to do better and get into better schools than mine or anyone else's child. They weren't about to be helpful with applications and that sort of thing. It also seemed to me," she confesses, "that everyone else had this under control and I was the only one whose life was in utter flux."

Try to find someone whose attitude toward the search is one you admire and would like to emulate. It doesn't hurt to ask upfront if this person would be willing to listen to your questions and complaints for the next few months. Look for someone who has a sympathetic nature, and remember, most people are flattered to be in the position of helping as long as they have the time to give you.

Your child's school may provide opportunities for you at least to chat with the other parents in the class. By all means take advantage of any teas, morning coffee sessions, or evening programs the school sets up. Support in any form will make it easier on you.

SEPARATING YOURSELF

As your child is preparing to leave the home front, you too have the opportunity, so to speak, to ease into having her leave. Many parents of teens started relinquishing more and more control as adolescence set in. If you haven't made that transition, this is an ideal time to begin. Don't dwell sadly on the fact that your child will be gone next year or the year after. "I'm not leaving for college for another year, but already my mom has started in on how much she's going to miss me," says a Cleveland junior in exasperation. "If I'm out for the day she'll say things like 'Next year you'll really be gone so I want as much of you as I can have now.' I mean really!"

Keep in mind that even though you find the thought of separation almost too painful, your child needs to flex his maturing muscles and you need to give him the chance to do so. He won't magically grow up when he's handed a high school diploma. Allowing him to navigate himself through the college search is an excellent place to start. "It's hard to separate yourself when you've been so close," admits the mother of a seventeen-year-old daughter. "My girl is quite an artist, something I would love to have pursued myself. My temptation is to push her toward a school that will give her a solid art background, but I am holding myself back. She has to decide that's what she wants for herself, not because I want it for her—or for me."

Should you hear yourself referring to the fact that "*We* are applying to school," let that be a signal that you are too involved. Period. *We* are not applying. Your child is applying. This can be tough for a successful parent to take. In most cases, people get to powerful positions by sheer dint of determination; it requires an equally herculean effort to keep yourself from attempting to determine your child's college fate.

Within the family unit, kids can be pulled in many directions. Dad wants one school, Mom wants another, and sometimes the fine schools brothers and sisters attended are tossed into the pressure blend. A Tulsa senior felt pulled in a direction he knew he couldn't go: "My brother was very successful and easily had his choice of colleges. I didn't have that kind of high school performance. I would have thought my parents expectations of me would be at my level, not my brother's. But they are obviously at his."

You can keep the whole thing from going out of control by being sure the focus is—and stays—where it belongs: on the child applying to college. This time is about finding out what will work best for him and discovering what schools are of the greatest interest and most appropriate to him. It is not an exercise in family pride or a test of how well you have raised your child. It is his search to locate the school he wants. As a wise high school senior put it: "Let your kids know that you can be proud of them and you love them even if they don't do what you want them to do. Be there for them and let them know you're ready to give your guidance if they need it. Give them enough room to stand on their own two feet, but enough space to fall back if they must. That way they'll learn from the fall."

There is life after college. In the sea of paperwork and the momentum that takes over during applications, you can lose sight of the fact that life's options continued for you after school ended, and they will for your child as well. With greater perspective you can more easily follow Dr. Perry's advice to all parents. "Your children want your support. They want you to know them well enough to recognize *their* needs and then help them meet those needs."

Chapter Three

SURVEYING THE FIELD

■■■■■■■■■■■■■■■■■■■■■■■■■■■■■■■■■■■■■■■

Absolutely the first question that enters everyone's mind when embarking on the college search is *Where?* With some 3,500 accredited colleges and universities in this country to choose from, finding *the* college could seem a staggering challenge. Fortunately, once the prospective student reaches some preliminary decisions, the field narrows quickly.

To some degree, you'll need to be the reality check for your student while establishing the list of college candidates. Teens can get carried away in their excitement about a school—not necessarily for an inappropriate one, and often for the wrong reasons. An older student comes home, sophisticated and giddy from his three months at Michigan, and, bingo, that's where your child "must" go. Or her friends have all decided that Oberlin is exactly the right school for them, and Oberlin becomes the decision of the day. Keep your head clear—and your sense of humor intact—and you can work out a college list that's just right. Don't, by the way, dismiss the schools that your child's friends are extolling. "It's not a bad way to start by listening to which schools are making friends happy. If the friends are similar in interests, likes, and dislikes, there's good reason to assume your child would like the same school, too," points out one consultant.

The operative word in deciding on a school is "comfortable." High school counselors talk about finding a school where the child will be comfortable. Parents who've been there remark how their child felt comfortable the moment she stepped on the campus. A Virginia dad recalls the rigorous experience he shared with his daughter as they searched for the right school: "Denise didn't want a school that was too hard although I think she could have done well at Brown, but then I'm her father. She had an opinion—a strong one—for every school we visited. At Middlebury she thought the students were working too hard. For reasons she couldn't explain, she was turned off by Colgate students. But when we got to Colby on the first spring day of the year and it was warm and students were playing Frisbee, she took one look and said, 'This is the place for me.' "

The sense of being comfortable is basically instinctive, and teens often have solid instincts. Denise's dad finishes his tale: "The irony is she never looked into the work ethic of the school, but she was right. It was exactly the right culture for her. She's been amazingly productive since she's been there, something she wasn't in high school." Listen to your child's feelings as you go about discussing schools and, as much as possible, pay personal visits to the campuses to strengthen immediate reactions. (More on campus visits in Chapter 4.)

As you start to decide which factors will play a role in determining the school list, the money issue needs special attention. It's a bit more complicated than you may think. If your family can't afford the high-scale schools, which are now easily $25,000 a year and more, your child's list should obviously have a generous selection of less expensive ones. But don't assume he can't apply to any schools with such stratospheric tabs. Add a few if they are schools that honestly interest your child. As you'll see in Chapter 7, financial aid comes in many sizes and shapes, and one could be the package that will see your child through an Ivy.

EARLY PICKS

As you begin the hunt, plan to come up with around fifteen schools to consider, twenty at most. From that rather long list, your child should ideally end up applying to six or so. "We're talking about something very personal," points out consultant Ronna Morrison. "There's no such thing as a 'good' school. It's what's really good for your child."

The list should contain one or two "reach" schools at which your child's admission is possible, maybe even probable, but hopeful; two or three very likely admissions; and two sure shots. Guidance counselors, private consultants, and college admissions experts agree that it's important to have at least a few schools where your child will almost certainly be accepted. This strategy practically guarantees a spot in a freshman class, but do be sure your child believes he would be happy at any one of his application schools, including his safety choices.

"Every April and May I hear from families I haven't met. Their story is the same," reports one busy consultant. "Their child got into only the safety school, and when they went to see it the child hated it." To prevent ending up with this scenario in your home, don't throw any school into the mix unless your child considers it a real possibility.

Similarly, don't have too many "reach" schools. Accompanying them, by definition, is the strong possibility of denial. Too many turn-downs will deflate your child's confidence, and that isn't good for any of you. Early in the process replace the word "rejection" with "denial." It carries a softer blow and is, indeed, closer to the truth. A student is not rejected, he is denied a place, sometimes merely because a school was looking for a fencer, a flutist, or a wrestler that year.

As you go about preparing the application list, bring up the subject of not being accepted along with other routine subjects. "I let my daughter know from the first that we expected her to be turned down by at least a few of the schools because this was a normal part of the process. She had the reassurance from the beginning that rejection in this case didn't mean anything about her or our feelings toward her," says a San Diego father.

Academics

Because your child is going to college ostensibly to learn, it's logical to start with the academic atmosphere and curriculum choices. If the teen knows at the outset that art is his calling and only a school with an excellent fine arts department will do, your job is cut out for you. Is your child looking for a strong math department, a school with excellent liberal arts, something with commercial specialties, or a good pre-med program? Is he the type for a rigorous academic climate, something less taxing, or, frankly, something quite easy? From his high school years you should have a clear grasp of your child's interests and strengths, and can help steer him toward the type of school curriculum that will meet his needs. A Tampa mother recalls with relief that her son was strongly interested in computer graphic design. "It narrowed the field for us right away. Even schools with good art departments were removed from the list if we found they didn't have a strong computer design department, too."

Students with a wide number of interests, however, are in the majority. These teens should look for liberal arts schools rather than institutes of technology. In most cases, colleges don't require students to declare a major until the end of sophomore year, and a school with a healthy variety of subject areas offers the chance to investigate a number of fields.

This is the time for you to be ruthlessly honest about your child's abilities and to evaluate fairly what she actually can and wants to do academically. You may have to lower your expectations some. A college that is too demanding could make her miserable. On the other hand, if your child has her heart set on a school you consider more difficult than she could handle, don't discourage it right away. Discuss her wishes with the high school counselor and weigh the strengths of the school—if it matches her strengths, it may be a good choice after all for reasons you don't know.

Although you may assume a larger school would automatically be more exciting academically, it isn't necessarily so. Sometimes a school gets its reputation more from the quality of its grad school than its undergrad departments. In large, prestigious schools the professors may teach only a few lectures a week, with graduate assistants bearing the bulk of the student-teacher load. A smaller school may demand more actual teaching on the part of its professors, prominent or otherwise, plus the lower student-professor ratio gives students a greater chance to interact with professors. If your child functions best in a small, nurturing environment, a smaller school with a strong academic program may be the best route.

Don't overlook your state schools either as strong academic contenders. Some, of course, such as many in the California system, have long-held outstanding academic reputations. The academic standards of others that have been less well thought of may have improved since the days you looked into colleges for yourself. With costs at many private colleges skyrocketing, state schools have become more attractive to zealous students, and the upgraded student body is helping some schools become better.

The new popularity of state schools is causing a different kind of problem: You can no longer assume that your own state school will guarantee a place for your child even though you are residents. Be sure your child applies early.

Social Climate

The next factor to weigh involves the social environment that best fits your child. Is yours a child who has numerous earrings and doesn't consider the weekend complete without hours spent hanging out in New York's Greenwich Village? This is not a student who would be happy mixing with Southern students on a small-town campus, a world apart from neon lights and liberal-leaning friends. Conversely, a student who prefers lots of open spaces and outgoing people probably shouldn't put Columbia, in the heart of Manhattan, or the University of Chicago on her list.

A more subtle aspect of the social climate is the nature of the student body. After all, it's likely that your child will make many of his lifelong friends on the college campus. He may well marry one of his fellow students. A laid-back Oregonian could be put off by the intensity of MIT students just as a driven New Yorker could be frustrated by the easygoing attitudes that prevail on some California campuses. Again, the word "comfortable" comes to mind. If the student body is made up of types similar to those your child relates to, his comfort level about the school will probably be high. On the other hand, your teen may welcome the new, the different, the unknown.

Location, Location, Location

Your fantasy may be that your child will select a school only a few hours from home. That way you can continue to see her on a somewhat regular basis, and she can come home for any important events. Her idea may be to go across the country to a place that is only hers, where she can forge her identity without the family on the fringes. Whatever the case, now is the time to get it all out on the table. "I was pleased when Margaret said she wanted to go someplace near family," recalls a divorced Denver mother about her junior in high school. "Then she explained it could be in New York with her aunt, or St. Louis with her dad. I just assumed when she said family she meant me," says the startled mother. An East Coast mother felt duped when her son, in keeping with her wishes that he not go farther than 500 miles away to school, selected one in rural Maine. "In good weather, the school is an eight-hour drive," his mother says, "but it's 'only' 375 miles away."

Location factors are more encompassing than the distance from family, though. Is your child a hot-weather fan or happy only with four definite seasons? Is he a skier who would consider the mountains that back the University of Colorado a piece of heaven, or is he a beach buff who would relish the nearby ocean at UCLA? He won't be studying all the time, and having appealing options of how to spend his off hours will enrich his overall college experience.

Finally, keep in mind transportation from home to school. If money is tight, the cost of airline tickets can strain the budget to the breaking point—or mean that your child won't get home more than once or twice a year. Also, if your child dislikes the process of traveling, guide her toward colleges that are close or that have direct travel routes.

The College Profile

When your child has made decisions concerning these matters, or at least has whittled them down to not more than several alternatives, it's time to make a college profile. He should write down an outline of the type of school he wants.

A profile might look like this:

- Academics: strong liberal arts, especially in political science, economics, and the like. Perhaps a good law school attached to its graduate program.
- Size: medium, at least 400 in the entering class, but not more than 800.
- Location: within 500 or so miles from home, warm climate. Prefer town of at least 10,000 or more people but not a city.
- Extracurricular: newspaper, drama.
- Social environment: somewhat conservative, students who are serious about learning.
- Fraternity/sorority system: not too powerful.
- Ethnic or religious preference: none.
- Dorms: coed.

FILLING IN THE LIST

Finding appropriate colleges that fit your child's profile calls for some investigation and creativity—or should. "There's a crush at the top because there are still too many parents who want prestige schools for their children," notes one high school guidance counselor in a New York school. Parents want one of perhaps 600 schools. This leaves 2,900 schools that don't get a flood of applicants, and one of these colleges may be exactly right for your child. Students can get a better, more appropriate education—in fact, a great one—in many, many places, not just the so-called top schools.

You can track down appealing candidates in a number of ways. The first, as mentioned, are the schools other students you know are attending. These students are up to date about their own schools and can give your child some first-hand information and insight. But your child should use word-of-mouth only as a starting point.

College Guidebooks, Nights, and Fairs

Your child's college profile will be invaluable as she tackles the candidate list in earnest. The first and easiest place to turn is to a good, comprehensive book listing colleges and their application requirements. The teen should check out at least several of the many available to find a format that is most comfortable for her to use. You should go through the books as well as you help her sort out—with the profile—what schools to consider. Your familiarity with a good guidebook's contents means you'll be able to discuss your child's questions about courses, majors, locations, athletics, and the like. Your knowledge can be comforting and encouraging, especially for the student who is reluctant, confused, or nearly paralyzed by the onslaught of information.

Computer software packages to help your student isolate schools of interest also are available. These are particularly useful for the student who doesn't have a clue about which schools she might want. She can input her profile, and the program will produce a list of possibilities for her. Many high schools have such programs. (See Resources for electronic options.)

It would be ideal if you could visit each school that's of interest to your child, but it's virtually impossible for most families. The college fair, then, becomes the closest thing to a visit and is a valuable shopping tool. The high school will know when and where college fairs are taking place; often the school itself is a sponsor. At the fair dozens of booths will be set up with material and representatives from various colleges.

To maximize efficiency at the fair, get a list of participating colleges in advance. Mark the booths of colleges that match your child's profile and go only to those. If no list is available, make up one of your own that has names of possible college candidates. If you try to do the fair in a more random fashion, you risk getting confused and bogged down with little to show for your visit.

Pick up material at your selected booths, including all application forms. This will spare you or your child the time and tedium of writing for forms later. If you need additional literature or forms, discuss it with the college rep on the spot, and he or she will arrange to send it to you when it's available.

The guidance counselor at your teen's high school will invite you to accompany your child to a college night, generally held in the middle of the junior year and fall of senior year. Sometimes programs are lead by the high school guidance office; sometimes by reps from a number of schools, by a financial director of a college, or by an independent financial consultant. These evenings are extremely valuable, and you shouldn't miss them. One high school, to give parents and students a greater understanding of how colleges select and how difficult it is to select among applicants, divided attendees into groups to act as admissions officers. Three fictitious applications were distributed for each group to ponder. Says one father about the evening: "It was a real eye-opener for us to see what did and didn't matter on the applications when we looked at them from the college's viewpoint. It also helped us realize that for the colleges, who gets in isn't personal; it's who fits best for that particular school." (The Appendix contains three fictitious applications and instructions if you would like to try this informative exercise with your child or by yourself.)

BEWARE THE SALES PITCH

You may be astonished by the razzle-dazzle colleges are using to sell themselves to potential students. Competition for applicants, except among very top-name schools, has become more intense, and schools, eager to enhance their appeal, have turned to the experts. Universities and colleges routinely hire professional advertising and public relations agencies, marketing organizations, and top-flight photographers to design printed materials, produce videos, and other "sell" pieces as well as plan overall strategy. One college rep proudly announced that his school's video "won the top award." Never mind that the graphic honor had nothing whatsoever to do with the quality of the school.

It's easy to be swayed by beautiful videos and powerful presentations. Campus videos offer a sense of place, but they cannot replace the information in the catalog and a visit before admission to the campus. Here is where you can be particularly helpful to your student. As an adult, you have more sophistication to sort out what really matters. Keep your critical eye open to help your teen cut through clever ploys and enticing designs. The last thing your teen needs is to be "lulled" into making a decision as critical as her college choice. Use the razzle-dazzle as an introduction only. Follow up with an investigation that allows you and your child to form opinions independent of snazzy marketing.

One other reminder about marketing influences: Every year there are "hot" schools based on several different things. *Newsweek* and *U.S. News & World Report* have annual "best colleges" lists that start a feeding frenzy. If a college receives extensive media coverage one year, usually for sports achievements, it generally receives an inordinate number of applications as a result. For instance, the year that a Syracuse University football player won the highly prized Heisman Trophy, the number of males applying to Syracuse doubled the following year. "Hot" schools are fine, but only if they meet your child's real needs.

EXPANDING THE OPTIONS

Although the majority of college-bound seniors follow the usual route and time frame (see Resources for a typical time line), other options may better suit some students. One student may want to pursue early admissions or early decision; another may need an alternative entrance path because of poor grades or test scores. Still others may find a junior or community college or, for the time being, no college at all a better choice.

Early Decision

A big-city lawyer reports with pride and astonishment how his daughter decided she wanted to go to Cornell's college of chemical engineering. "She was so sure about this," he recalls, "that she obtained all the papers and sent them in without even telling me." He was even more astonished and pleased when, at the time many students were still applying for and to their schools, his daughter had gained entry into Cornell's freshman class. She did this through the process called early decision.

For early decision, the student may apply to various schools, but he agrees that he will attend his early decision school if admitted—a decision that will generally be reported by the college before December 15. (This gives the student time to make any additional applications before the January 1 deadline many schools require.) There is one important reminder concerning early admissions: Many high school students change their minds about what school they want more or less constantly. Any student applying for an early decision should be confident (and so should his parents) that this is definitely the school for him since it carries that commitment with it.

A student who is denied acceptance initially is reconsidered typically later in the year along with those applying in the usual time frame. However, early decision candidates may want to follow the route advised by Rona Kole, head of a public school guidance office. "Over the years, many of our early decision candidates have backup applications filled out and ready for the mail in case they're turned down at their first-choice college."

39

Early Admissions

This admission process is reserved for exceptional juniors who, should they be accepted into college, would skip their senior year of high school. They enter college in what would have been their senior year as freshmen. Qualifications and provisions for early admissions may differ from school to school and year to year. Carefully check the current requirements for the college in question.

Early Action

Yet another form of speeding up the process is called early action. The schedule for application is the same as for early decision, that is, usually by November 1, but acceptance is not binding. Students receive notification in December and generally have until May 1 to notify the school about their plans. An early action candidate who is turned down may not reapply to the school. This option is being phased out by many schools.

Rolling Admissions

Rolling admissions describes a process in many schools that allows students to apply whenever they wish before a final deadline. (You may have to ask exactly when that is.) The college continues to accept students as they apply—and continues to do so until all the available spaces are filled. This process is particularly helpful to students getting a late start in applications. Rolling admissions colleges usually respond in four to six weeks' time.

Deferred Admission

Once admitted, a student who received deferred admission has a choice to delay enrolling for a semester or even an entire year. A deposit to hold a space in the appropriate class may be requested, and the student may have to substantiate how he spent the deferred period of time.

Athletes' Choices

If your child is destined to become an athletic star—and remember, only 1 in 10,000 high school basketball players go on to play pro ball—college coaches in the sport have long had their eye on him. College scouts watch for high school superstars in the sports offered by the college. If your child is an exceptional player, he won't need to worry about finding schools, they'll find him—and you.

For the overwhelming majority of high school athletes, however, there is more work involved in locating a college that offers an appealing sports program. Several software packages have information on sports programs at various schools. There are also guidebooks for this purpose. (See Resources.) Your child should discuss possible college choices with his or her high school coach as well.

Junior and Community Colleges

"There was no way my son was ready to be serious about his education when he graduated from high school," observes a mother in Albuquerque. "He needed something between high school and college that would keep him involved in the educational system but didn't demand the commitment of most universities." This family decided on a nearby junior college, a successful choice, as it turned out. "After a year there, Tom had matured enough to focus on his schooling. He went on to the University of Utah and is doing well. In fact, he's thinking about medical school," says his mother.

Junior or community college is an excellent choice for many students who want a sort of holding ground. Going to a more demanding university may hurt a student's long-range prospects if she isn't ready to tackle studying in a meaningful way. If she ends up having to leave one university, the poor grades that caused her departure may keep her from being able to transfer to other schools where she would do well.

Community colleges—there are some 1,200 of them—are also a strong possibility for students who want to be close to home or with mediocre records. They are a fine solution as well for students who want to save money or who prefer to move quickly into the job market and can do so with an associate degree in their chosen field. For those who wish to continue their higher education, many junior and community colleges have agreements with four-year schools that allow students to matriculate automatically after completing the two-year program. Be sure to look into which schools are affiliated if your child is considering this option.

A note to skeptics: A recent study prepared jointly by Princeton and Harvard professors for the National Bureau of Economic Research showed that the estimated per-credit value in returns (i.e., dollars earned) was quite similar for graduates of two-year and four-year colleges.

Alternate Admissions

Say your child doesn't have either the high school grades, the SAT or ACT scores to get into the school he wants. There may be an option for him to gain admission in spite of his poor records. Some universities offer alternative admissions in these cases. Typically, the student must attend summer school, either on the university's own campus or another determined or approved by the school. Admission to the university in question is based on the student's earning a stipulated grade point average.

Some schools, usually public colleges and universities,

have conditional admission status: A student matriculates with the understanding that she will take courses—not for college credit—to make up specific deficiencies in her high school academic record. Other colleges offer alternate admissions via the previously mentioned arrangement with a community or junior college.

Alternate admissions practices change a great deal even from year to year. If such a program is of interest to your child, look into any and all options thoroughly and be sure your informant's material is up to date. Having a clear map for alternate admissions could, according to Stacy Needle, author of *The Other Route into College: Alternative Admission*, "mean the difference between acceptance and nonacceptance into college." It also can make the difference in the type of college your child enters—whether it is the competitive college of choice or one that is only marginally acceptable.

A Year "On"

You may have a child who has announced a nonintention about college. You know—"I have no intention of going to college—at least this year." Before you tear your hair, give some thought to the following.

Not everyone, including academic superstars, has to go to college right after high school. Some students are not emotionally ready to begin college, whether because of the academic commitment it requires or their reluctance to leave home and the familiar. Many students want freedom from academic pressure for a year, or they look forward to starting college with more maturity. "I think I'll enjoy college a lot more and do better there because I'm taking a year to grow up a little first," says a determined senior who bucked her parents to delay college.

43

"Not going to school for a year is a child's option that many parents don't even consider," admits Ronna Morrison, an educational consultant. "I think parents are frightened that if the child doesn't go immediately after high school, the child will never go," she adds. It's understandable that parents feel this way, but former university provost, college dean, and educational consultant Dodge Johnson maintains that delaying college entry is the right decision for some students. Students who truly hate school and never got academics together in four years of high school probably aren't ready for college. Sometimes working for a year or two earning $6 to $8 an hour is enough to convince a teen that college and the promise of the better job a degree offers is the way to go.

Interestingly, while parents refer to a year between high school and college as a year "off," educators think of it as a year "on." In Morrison's experience, students who begin college without sound motivation, who had parents who pushed them into going to college and did most of the work to get them there, are the students most likely to fail, to be put on probation, or to drop out of school without a degree. It may take that year "on" for these students to become ready for college.

Chapter Four

COLLEGES CLOSE UP: VISITS AND INTERVIEWS

■■

You wouldn't move into a new house without looking into every nook and cranny. You wouldn't buy a car without taking it out for a spin. And you shouldn't expect your child to select the place where he's going to spend the next four years, the institution that will become a part of his life résumé, without looking it over. An on-campus visit is an invaluable way for students to form opinions—sometimes uncannily accurate ones—about their comfort level at any given school.

Guidance director Anne Franzese reports she has seen the following situation time and time again: "A child who thought he was going to love a school drives up to the campus and doesn't even want to get out of the car. He knows something isn't right for him. In contrast, there's the child who didn't think she would like a certain college, sees it, and falls in love with it." Students seem to know from the briefest encounters that they belong . . . or don't.

Colleges also are concerned that students have seen their campus when they apply. An important number for colleges is their "yield," that is, the number of acceptances they receive in relation to the number of acceptances they send out. For marketing purposes, obviously they want their yield numbers to be high. A student who has visited the campus, seen the good *with* the bad, and still wants to enter that school is more apt to say yes than a student who applies "blind." Admissions offices know this for a fact. So the applicant who paid a visit may have an advantage over the one who didn't in the college's decision-making process.

Sometime in your child's junior year, if not before, start dropping by campuses in your area and in any other areas you may be visiting. You can survey a good number of them by making a campus stop or two part of a weekend, long weekend, or vacation. If at all possible, go to a variety of schools, urban and rural, small and large. Once your child has met with college reps at college fairs or her high school's college nights, she probably will have a more focused idea of the schools she most wants to see. By her senior year, she'll have her college profile ready, and she'll have spoken with a number of reps and student friends at different colleges. Then it's time to get serious about visits.

PLAN AHEAD

The summer before your child's senior year, you may need to set aside the weeks you normally would go on a family vacation for driving around to college campuses, especially if he is involved in sports or other activities that make it difficult to get away during the school year. It's preferable, however, to visit during the school year, when students are everywhere in evidence. Your child will have a chance to hang out in the dorms and the gym. Having a chance to size up his peers will give him much of the insight he needs to formulate his thoughts about a school.

When you have a travel plan, incorporate as many campuses as possible. Tack an extra Friday or Monday onto a weekend. One mother reports she and her son were able to complete the visits in a weekend. "Ben was interested in only four schools, all nearby. We drove off on Friday, and by Sunday afternoon, we were finished," she says.

A father remembers campus touring quite differently. "My daughter had no idea what she wanted in a school and we ended up going to seventeen different campuses. This took us weeks and weeks," he notes.

Whatever your total, call the admissions offices to find out what kind of guidance they can give. Many schools offer formal or informal tours, often led by students. Some schools have an open-door policy, meaning you may visit any time. Others maintain specific times for visits. Call ahead to maximize your visit and to avoid disappointment.

Once on campus, it can be useful for the two or three of you to wander about separately. Not only does it give you the advantage of seeing more and comparing notes later, it also gives your child a chance to absorb what she is seeing and the atmosphere strictly on her own without being influenced by anything her parent says—or thinks. The tour should include a dorm or two, the student union, dining halls, a classroom, lecture halls, and, if you can and your child is interested, a fraternity or sorority house. Read material on bulletin boards as you go around and chat with as many students as possible. It's through these campus conversations and wanderings that you and your child will discover what gives a college its flavor.

Remind your child that in these next four years she will be getting much more than her academic degree. She should think seriously about the kind of social life she wants, the type of people she prefers as friends, the level of politics and activism that interests her—and keep all of these things in mind as she rubs shoulders with students on each campus you see.

To get more from your campus visits when months later you're struggling with memory problems, such as where you saw some particular building or scene, take lots of pictures, especially of those things that don't appear in the college brochure. The town's main street, the dorm rooms, and the dining hall are relevant photo subjects. Be discreet as you travel from building to building. Since your child probably would rather die than to be with a parent who is photographing the campus, plan to do this on your own. Have the photos developed quickly and mark each clearly for your records.

INTERVIEW INFO

It's best to keep the campus visit and the interview separate occasions, if feasible. Interviews, almost by definition, are hand-wringing events, and the nervousness can cloud a campus visit. Again, check into interviewing policies. A few of the large universities and sought-after schools no longer do on-campus interviews, but they will arrange for an alumnus in your area to conduct one with your child. This gives students an opportunity to get that part of the process out of the way on their home turf. Some colleges have reps interview when they visit high schools. Many colleges, because of reductions in admissions staff, schedule only group interviews. If this is the case, insisting on an individual interview can raise a negative flag for your applicant.

If the college does offer individual interviews, even if the school's forms state "interviews optional," be sure your child has one. Colleges assume that students who are most interested will go to the trouble of being interviewed. One college guidance counselor recalls two applicants with equally strong qualifications seeking a place at the same small but competitive school. "One student made sure she had an interview. The other didn't bother since the school said it wasn't necessary. All I know is that the one who interviewed got in, and the other didn't." The implication is clear. If distance precludes a personal interview, the college will note that. If distance doesn't, the college will note that too. But check to see if a local alumnus can conduct an interview anyway.

Making the appointment is one case in which you may step in for your child. "It doesn't matter which of you sets up the interview," says admissions director Delsie Phillips. Students aren't around phones during the day as much as their parents are, and colleges know that. Obviously, having your secretary call is too impersonal.

Don't drag out your teen's blue blazer and rep tie for an interview. College officials, of all people, understand student dress today. Stress neatness and an appropriately formal look, but don't be alarmed if your student's choice is more casual than whatever you have in mind. Remember too that part of the college's purpose in conducting interviews is to sell the college. You may be able to soothe your child's nerves by mentioning that. As a whole, college interviewers are friendly. They want you to like their schools.

Some students arrive at the interview ready to talk about and show everything they've done since second grade. "It's great to see the progression of their skills and talents," notes one college interviewer, "but I'd rather spend the time discovering where the student is now." However, your child should consider the potential content of the interview before she gets there. The high school guidance office will have typical questions admissions people ask. But as an admissions director who has interviewed thousands of students warns, "It's a mistake to prep students too much for interviews. They lose their spontaneity and they get scared. They don't behave naturally," he observes.

Drilling will just make your child more nervous, but you should underscore the following points:

- •Has she read the college literature? She doesn't want to ask questions that have answers clearly outlined in the college brochure.
- •She should have two or three questions ready whose answers aren't in the college's materials.
- •If she has a good idea about what her major will be, some questions should address aspects of that department, such as particular areas of strength.
- •If she's really anxious, she should think about the worst questions that could be asked. No one ever asks them.

Remind her as well that she should take the opportunity to be honest about a poor grade during a difficult period. She'll be more relaxed knowing she doesn't have to skirt around some grades on her transcript. A frank assessment of what was going on at the time, perhaps family issues or health concerns, may be just the item that sets her interview apart from the others and makes her memorable.

*　*　*

Once you arrive at the interviewer's office, let your child take over. Don't be the one to announce your arrival—"I'm here with my child John for the eleven o'clock interview"— let your teen announce himself. Otherwise it gives the impression that he is overly dependent on you. You can avoid any tendency to speak for your child by locating the admissions building or office and sending him in alone.

"Parents often want to have a sort of preliminary interview in which they tell us all the good things about their child," says an admissions interviewer. "Kids are good at taking care of this themselves, and the parents must let them do it." You may be particularly concerned about your child if he is shy, but remember that interviewers are trained to work with a variety of personalities. They know how to bring out the shy student.

There is no such thing as the "wrong" answer, a fact that may be of comfort to your child. Interviewers are trying to find out what kind of person your child is, the qualities he has that make him unique and special as well as the nature of his personality. Is he dynamic or gentle, magnetic or sensitive? There are going to be times when the interviewer and your child don't hit it off. That's natural, but that too is nothing to worry about. Says Delsie Phillips: "It's not possible for a student to have an affinity for every interviewer he meets. If he expresses an opinion or gives an answer that isn't in keeping with the institution, then it's likely to be the wrong place for him anyway."

Throughout campus visits and interviews, don't lose sight of the weight your opinions carry with your teen. As much as she may deny caring what you think, your child listens to you—what you say matters. Give your opinion only if asked. Geraldine Fryer, among other consultants, feels parents should provide only meals and wheels for these excursions. "If you start saying things like 'This is a good place for you,' or it isn't, you'll muddy the waters for your child. She might turn against it because you like it. Let her form her own impressions and make up her own mind," she stresses.

Chapter Five

DOWN TO BUSINESS
■■■■■■■■■■■■■■■■■■■■■■■■■■■■■■■■■■■■■■

Getting your teenager off to college represents a seismic shift in your relationship, as the power that has always been yours moves to your child. Through the months ahead, your child will begin to get the sense of self that she must have to live apart from the family successfully. Most colleges have an orientation program to ease students through the transition between "home rule" and self-rule. But, Amy Costello, assistant director of admissions of Lehigh University, explains, "The students who do best are the ones who were given reasonable freedom and responsibilities to learn how to manage their time *before* their freshman year of college."

In numerous ways, the college search itself will contribute not only to your child's budding maturity but also to his ability to manage his schedule and work load. There is a large amount of work to tackle, more, perhaps than he has ever confronted before. In a few months' time he'll have to obtain and complete applications, write essays, locate and arrange for recommendations, take SATs or ACTs, consult with experts, visit campuses, and probably be interviewed. That's a lot for anyone, especially a sixteen- or seventeen-year-old. From these tasks and experiences, your child will go far in developing important personal assets; he'll learn more about how to organize himself, how to meet deadlines, and how to present himself in a confident fashion. The manner in which your child handles the search can propel him toward true adulthood.

If he brings himself through this saga to a successful outcome, he will leave home with confidence that will help him handle college, the next major situation in his life, and then the next. He has proved to himself (and perhaps to you) that he doesn't need Mom or Dad to be successful, he is capable of succeeding on his own terms.

YOUR CONTINUING ROLE

So where, you wonder, does this leave you? Expect to take some time to work out just what your input will be in this lengthy process. Every family finds its own balance. But overall, the best way to describe a parent's role is that of invaluable assistant. Your assistance isn't limited to offering two hands, ready to pitch in collating papers; you are the kind of aide you treasure in your own work life. You assist by being in the know: where to get information, and how to pin down things.

You're also the wise adviser and the enthusiastic cheerleader. Guidance director Anne Franzese describes the parent's role as this: "The ideal parent is one who is supportive, aware of all the stress, aware of how difficult this is for the child, yet enables the child to do it on her own. But the parent is there, in the background holding everything together."

Don't underestimate your importance to your teen. In spite of the confidence and independence many teens like to project, most of them find the prospect of applying to college overwhelming and the thought of leaving the family downright terrifying. As parent, you play a major role—emotionally and practically—during this period of your child's life. No matter how much she may profess not to need your help, she both wants and needs it. It's ironic that, as a mother of a high school junior points out, "The college search coincides with the point in teens' lives when they don't want to know from their parents. But if something doesn't work out," this savvy mother adds, "you know what their first reaction always is. 'Why didn't you tell me?' and they look straight at you."

GETTING STARTED

Although undoubtedly it is on your child's mind, probably you will actually bring up the loaded word first: college. Initiate the discussion while there is still plenty of time to mull the subject over, ingest it in bits and pieces, and finally get some energy behind it. That means preferably starting to talk about college early during your child's junior year, but certainly no later than the first month of senior year. Start by telling your teen that you understand this is a difficult and stressful experience and that it may involve some volatile feelings. Then ask what she would like your involvement in the search to be. How best, and how much, can you help her? Give her time to think it over, but don't leave it hanging. Establish right at the onset a date for a week or two hence to discuss her master plan.

You really can't anticipate how much parental input your child will want. Teens differ widely in their preferences. In high school group discussions, some kids were frank that they wanted their parents to "stay out of business that isn't theirs." Others, though, hoped parents would be right there, "to make sure I do it right." Yours may be a teen who is fiercely independent and would perceive your help as an intrusion, or you may have one who wants you guiding her through the entire process. You have to ask. Then you have to watch. Don't be shy about articulating your observations about your child's progress and feelings as you go along. If you think she is beginning to resent you, ask. You'll both feel better if you address—and if necessary correct—the situation. Plus it will set the stage for an overall easier give-and-take throughout the search months—or year.

Painful though it may be, you'll have to live with the fact that what your child wants from you may well not be what you'd like to give. One mother, from Chicago, remains almost bitter about the conflict she had with her son. "I knew he could get in to anyplace he wanted with a moderate amount of effort. But he wasn't willing to exert himself. He is so disorganized, which bothered me a lot because I'm just the opposite. I tried to help him out, but he wouldn't let me. He kept saying 'Leave me alone, I have everything under control.' My only comfort was that maybe this would be a good lesson about consequences for him."

For your prearranged appointment with your teen, bring a list of the guidelines you need to establish. The first, of course, is your teen's preference for your input. Discuss this in detail and be sure both of you are clear and in agreement about your participation. Assuming your child wants you in, your first task together is to set up the all-important schedule. Work out a list of what you must accomplish and prepare a time line that covers all deadlines. Be sure to include review courses and standardized testing dates. The schedule will be bookended by the final date to write for applications and the final dates to mail them to schools. In between will be dates for visiting campuses, filling out applications, writing essays, requesting recommendations, checking that these have been sent in, along with the other minutiae of college applications. Add to your list which of you will be responsible for what. A blank calendar in your teen's room with large date boxes filled in with proposed dates and deadlines helps to keep the process moving smoothly. (See Resources for a sample time line.)

You can teach your child an invaluable skill by helping her understand the schedule. Controlling this process is simply breaking down a big job into manageable parts, thus creating an efficient work flow—a skill she will value in college and in every job she'll ever have. Unless yours is one of the rare teens who doesn't procrastinate, you will want to build some breathing room into this particular schedule. One reason a Los Angeles mother built so much time into her son's schedule, she says, was so that she and her husband didn't "get sucked into doing any more that we had to." She continues that they "didn't want to spend that year jumping from crisis to crisis. My son had a tough first-semester senior year coming up, so to make sure he had enough time to do a good job on his applications we set the first deadline as Labor Day. We then distributed the rest of the work load to fit most easily around his schedule. Even so, my husband and I checked in with him regularly to be sure he wasn't getting backed up."

Check-in time is, in fact, an important part of the process in all families. Make this a time that is separate from the day-to-day family functions, especially meals. In fact, do yourselves, your entire family, and your digestive tracts a favor by officially banning college discussions from the dinner table. Decide instead to hold a regular meeting on the subject once a week rather than daily, after your child returns from a full day of school. Sunday afternoon from three to four might work for you, or perhaps a weekday evening.

Establish a regular agenda for your check-in sessions, much as you would expect for a staff meeting in an office. Review what has been done, what needs to be done, and what is pressing. Make it clear to your child that she is free to express uncertainties or doubts about anything, from the colleges she is considering to how you are handling your end of things. If she needs more from you, encourage her to speak up. Encourage her equally if she is harboring second thoughts about your involvement in her search. Make it a goal to keep these regular meetings free of strife—it's good practice for both of you to listen to each other without judging or taking anything personally.

THE PROCESS BEGINS

Once your child signs up for the PSATs, ACTs, or the SATs, his name goes on a multitude of lists and you will get mail. Lots of mail. One mother says, "The mailbox hasn't been the same since. Everyday we pull out envelope after envelope, all pertaining to college. We're getting buried in the stuff."

There is a way to get around being overwhelmed by mail stacked up around your home. Do as an Arizona parent did with her son. Keep at hand the profile of the types of schools that might be of interest (see Chapter 3), ranging from geographical location to size, diversity to cost, acceptance rates and policies, *anything* that you've determined could influence the decision to go there. "With my son's college profile in hand," she recalls, "we knew as catalogs came in whether to keep them. We dumped the ones that didn't qualify instantly to get them out of the way. We then made a holding pile for the ones that had possible interest along with the primary pile of ones definitely of interest. It kept the incoming mail manageable and also gave us a jump on organizing the colleges Alan was most likely to want."

Early on—in the spring of the junior year or September of the senior year, you probably will have your first official meeting with the school college guidance counselor, a person who will play a powerful role in your student's life during the next six months to a year. If a meeting is not scheduled, request one. The counselor's involvement can be to everyone's advantage—no matter how much you think you know about colleges, the counselor almost always knows more. Needless to say, you'll benefit from having a compatible relationship with this person. (Chapter 6 contains a complete discussion of the high school counselor's role.)

Listen carefully and let the counselor and student steer the meeting and do most of the talking. These two will be meeting a lot in the next months, and they need to establish a working relationship independent of you. You also may find by observing more and talking less that you can spot any potential conflicts counselor and child might have, whether of personality or approach. If you need to talk with the counselor on your own, he or she will be readily available to you over the course of the year. On the other hand, your child may be handling this end so well you may have no reason ever to see the counselor again.

Occasionally, the high school counselor becomes set on a particular school or group of schools for your child. This is a problem of course, only if you or your child disagrees with the recommendations, but in that case it can become a sensitive issue. Try not to get riled up, even when you are truly upset. Instead, contain your feelings and explain your position rationally. This keeps emotions under control and creates a cordial environment in which the counselor will keep working hard, advocating for your child. There is yet another reason not to churn hostile feelings between you and the counselor. This person will be writing a letter of recommendation to accompany your child's applications, and his or her judgment will influence admissions officers. Obviously, you want this person to have positive feelings when your family name comes up. (More on recommendation letters follows.)

Should the counselor select an unwieldy number of choices for your child, or if the counseling itself isn't up to par, you can help by paying close attention to the suggested college list. Evaluate if the schools correspond closely to your child's interests and what you understand her abilities to be. You'll be especially valuable to her if you're informed and you stay calm.

APPLICATION TIME

Finally it's time to fill in the blanks. The application forms can be both detailed and demanding. The level of thought, creativity, and simple neatness that makes for a quality application can tempt nearly any parent to go into the all-powerful mode that was appropriate in the toddler years, but certainly not with a teen. Yes, you do have the maturity and savvy to turn applications into works of art that will astonish the admissions officers. "I wanted to take it to the office with me, to edit it, and have my colleagues look it over," admits a San Francisco mother. "It was all I could do to let my daughter do it herself." But she did and, of course, so will you.

One parent, respecting her son's territory, reduced the tedium for him by filling in the "boring" biographical data. "It's pretty much the same thing over and over," she notes. "I saved him time. I didn't see any benefit in having him write his birth date and address again and again."

Increasingly students are using computer software programs to help with the initial search and to simplify the task of completing applications. Your child can input his "particulars" just once; the programs include space for the essay. (See Resources.) Well over 700 public and private institutions are accepting computer-generated applications. Among them are Harvard, Duke, Stanford, and the Universities of Vermont, Wisconsin, Colorado, and Alabama, to name just a few. Your child should at least consider such a method for some of his applications.

For standard ones, parents can have some impact in assuring the applications will be more impressive. No one could argue with the following simple precaution and step toward perfection: photocopy the applications before your child fills them in. The copies are the place for mistakes, smudges, erasure marks, and late-night giddy responses.

Your informational input also can make the difference between an application that gets tossed and one that intrigues. As your child is compiling data for the applications, sit with him to review pertinent parts of his background. Who better than you recalls the awards, hobbies, sports, clubs, and other activities that your child was involved in during the growing-up years? Additionally, you may have a stronger sense about what will interest and impress a college and you can guide your child in recalling those things that show real student potential.

When your child has completed applications to her satisfaction, ask if you may review them for spelling, grammar, and the usual other things that you probably have more practice at seeing and correcting. If you are also the better typist, you might then opt, with your child's permission, to get the typewriter out of mothballs and do the typing. Be prepared for a secondary temptation while typing: to edit material as you go. A little tailoring here and there may strike you as a good idea, but are the changes what your child really wants? More to the point, it is imperative that the responses reflect the applicant's true feelings and thoughts. Colleges want to see what the student is really about, not what her parents think they want to see.

THE APPLICATION ESSAY

One of the most important parts of the application is your child's essay. Colleges want the student to express her feelings, ideals, and goals as well as explain more about who she is and whom she hopes to become. The essay is the applicant's direct voice to admissions committee members; through it your child has the opportunity—one of the very few—to make herself a real person to them, one they will care about. "The essay should show growth without saying 'I grew,' " explains educational consultant Dodge Johnson. "You want the admissions people to remark, after reading your essay, 'We want this person.' Most good essays tell a story—it may not be the whole thing, but there will be a story in there somewhere. Stories catch people's hearts. It's much harder to turn down people than it is to turn down folders.''

That kind of personal writing is difficult for just about anyone. The urge to write the essay for your child will be particularly compelling—or to get someone who does write well to do it. Some parents go so far as to hire professionals for the application essay. "I was horrified when I was asked by a father to write his son's essay," reports an image consultant and speechwriter in New York. "I told him I was appalled at the suggestion, but I know he'll keep calling around until he finds someone who agrees to do it."

At first glance it is daunting to think of your child's essay, the words of a seventeen-year-old, competing with thoughts and images presented by a professional writer. Take comfort, then, from the observation of college consultant who has been working with students and universities for several decades. "Admissions officers see thousands of essays and they know very well from the courses taken, the transcript, and responses to the other application sections on what level the student writes. When an essay comes in that is more evocative of F. Scott Fitzgerald than of the high school senior in question, you can bet their suspicions go up. The essay will be especially suspect if the quality of the rest of the application doesn't back up that of the essay," she notes. If indeed the total application isn't in sync, admissions people go looking for other discrepancies, they report. They'll be looking at your child's application with the intent of finding out what's *wrong* with it, a terrible position for an applicant to be in.

Certainly you should ask to review your child's essays before they go into final form. You may want to give suggestions about how best to organize and structure them. Your stress should be on guiding your child in presenting her thoughts in a lucid fashion, advises Corey Vigdor, assistant academic dean of St. Peter's College in New Jersey. "Colleges look to see if a student has the ability to formulate her ideas clearly," he reports.

On the other hand, you shouldn't suggest too many changes or you'll take away the buoyancy that is characteristic of many teens' writing styles. "Tampering too much with an essay ends up hurting it," observes educational consultant Ronna Morrison. "It loses its spontaneity, its humor, and the real part of the child." Morrison suggests your child retain a copy of the essay in its original words, before any polishing or rewrite. Then after editing and fine-tuning, check the finished draft against the original. "It's easier to bring life back into an essay that has been overcorrected when you have something to return to," she explains.

Overwriting also can become a problem when students prepare their college essays in high school English classes. Some teachers assign the college essay early in senior year, and then students, as busy as Santa's elves, work away to make it increasingly impressive. They load it with profound thinking and SAT vocabulary words. And they end up with a stifled and stifling essay, stripped of the impressive edge they had hoped to relate. If your child is writing her essays in school, again, have her keep her original words and store them away to bring balance back into an overblown composition.

Writer's block may set in while your child is struggling to put thoughts into words. You might help by making suggestions about ways to tailor the required topic to your child's interest and experiences. Let's look at an essay question that asks about a teen's career goals. She's stumped immediately. But wait, you can ask her to consider why she wishes to attend college; what are her areas of interest; talk about part-time jobs she has held, volunteer work she has done, her talents. She may view college as an opportunity to explore several career directions or to home in on one. Help her figure out why she is leaning in one direction or another. What influenced her—a person, a job, an experience; what drives her toward a specific career? Probe what she expects to gain from her career path and what she thinks she can offer. Brainstorm for real events, people, circumstances, and feelings that are propelling your student. You may need more than one session together to get concrete responses going.

It may be useful to have your child start by "talking it over" into a tape recorder. Speaking is generally easier than writing, and taping his thoughts might warm him up sufficiently to get him going. Be sensitive if the subject matter requested or the one he chooses is more personal than your child is comfortable having you see or hear. If this is the case, reassure him that you won't snoop about the essay— and stick to your promise.

Many universities accept what is called the common application, which is a single form. (See Appendix.) By using the common application, students may use the same essay or personal statement repeatedly, as they do all the other information on the form. However, it is unlikely that all schools on your child's list will accept the common application, and some may require individual essays. Essay-writing, at that point, could turn into a full-time project. If your child is allowed to select the topic of the essay, he probably can get good mileage from the original essay because the topics are general and usually appropriate for most schools. With a little editing and change of slant, he can adapt his original from the common application for use on applications to other schools, or vice versa. As a parent you may be better able than your teen to see the possibilities for doing so, especially since he is apt to be panicked by the volume of pending work.

THIS KID'S GREAT!
GETTING THE BEST REFERENCE LETTERS

Most colleges request a recommendation letter from the high school counselor, two teachers, and one "outside" letter. If the school counselor has a large number of students, have your teen prepare a list of significant achievements— both in and out of school—and major interests for the counselor to refer to when writing his recommendation.

An additional source of information for the counselor is the letter many of them ask parents to write as a "recommendation" for their child. Although it may not be stated directly, a counselor is looking for insights into your child's strengths and weaknesses that would affect college performance. The counselor will use some, most, or all of your input to complete his recommendation or school report to the colleges on behalf of your child. Don't worry about the formality or correctness of your comments. This is your chance to boast and, if necessary, to explain, and it's a great opportunity to advance your child indirectly without infringing on her territory. Give concrete examples of your child's originality or creativity (a play she developed for children's theater), leadership ability (a volunteer effort she spearheaded), and intellectual curiosity (she read much of Shakespeare before it was required). Be sure to include any extenuating circumstances at home that she has had to assist with, adjust to, or overcome. Note unique personality traits that might not be evident to teachers and other school staffers—her sense of humor, zest for life, empathy, independence, and so forth. Respond quickly and thoroughly to this request. All answers are confidential, and counselors destroy your comments after putting the information to use.

Some colleges accept extra letters if they add new information about the applicant not covered elsewhere in the application package. Check each application carefully for attitudes toward additional letters of praise, and use your judgment about which references will be most valuable in bringing your child to life for the admissions committee. Letters offer colleges insight into the way others view the student. These observations and opinions give recommendation letters a unique value among the application papers. You and your student should give careful consideration before enlisting the "others." A young woman who lived in a small western town was astonished to discover the neighbors she asked to write one of her letters gave her a lukewarm evaluation. "I found out too late that they were against my going to college so far away. It was their way of subtly sabotaging a decision they disagreed with!" Fortunately, she was accepted in spite of the letter of faint praise, but others haven't been so lucky.

A good letter should give the admissions readers a strong sense of the applicant's motivation, sense of responsibility, dependability, ability and willingness to work hard, and other traits that make for successful students. To achieve such a letter, guide your child toward teachers, coaches, school advisers, or employers who you know are enthusiastic about him. If the request is met with hesitation, look elsewhere for letter writers. For those who do agree, your child should have a page or two (perhaps the one he may have prepared for his guidance counselor) outlining his activities, interests, hobbies, school performance, employment, and the like to make writing the letter a bit easier. The information may contain just what the person needs to use as examples to verify the fine characteristics she senses in your child.

Nota bene: People who are asked for letters by a number of students, such as teachers and counselors, have more enthusiasm and time to compose attention-getting missives early in the game. Give the recommendation letters priority status in your child's college search to take advantage of these people's energy before it begins to wane.

Here are other tips to keep the recommendation letters moving smoothly.

•Don't ask family friends to write letters unless they have spent a good deal of time around your child in the last year or so and can talk knowingly about her. This holds true even if the family friend is a senator or other prestigious figure. Admissions personnel reveal that many of the letter writers who know the family well but not the child are painfully honest. "We get letters telling us they haven't seen 'little Johnny' since he was a toddler, but that the family's great. That isn't going to help us in the least," points out one admissions officer. Some admissions directors do not like the implied interference in their professional role when they believe writers have been chosen *solely* because of their supposed influence—for instance, a successful, high-profile alum or high-powered public figure.

•Include stamped business-size envelopes addressed correctly to the colleges for which the letters are intended. This cuts down on the problem of getting letters to the mailbox on time.

•Include a stamped addressed postcard to your child. It should say the following: "Your letter of recommendation to (name of college) was mailed on_____." Put the name of the person writing the letter on the top for your own records. Include one card for each college that will be receiving a recommendation from that person. This cuts down on the annoyance and anxiety of having to call people to find out if they have mailed some or all of their letters. Remember that a brief follow-up thank-you note to all who sent in recommendations is a must for your child.

VIDEOS AND OTHER ADD-ONS: WHEN MORE MAY BE TOO MUCH

Parents sometimes are tempted to "make sure" colleges know all the impressive aspects of their child and so encourage her to add reams of other material along with the application papers. Part of the application challenge is to avoid overkill. For the most part, unrequested material is not only a waste of time but also an annoyance to college admission offices, already besieged by papers they must sift through and evaluate. Often it is more beneficial to show some supporting material to an interviewer. However, some of the time there may be exceptions. They are:

- •Art students wishing to submit slides of their work. Send one sheet of slides, preferably to the Art Department, which will forward it on to admissions.
- •A few newspaper clippings covering your student's accomplishments.
- •One short story for students interested in creative writing.
- •A video *if it is outstanding, original, and genuinely*

shows off a student's talents that cannot be realized from other pieces of the application. Many colleges do not accept videos ever and would resent seeing one in your child's application package. In fact, at least one admissions director calls videos the "biggest no-no there is." That puts sending a video on shaky ground at the very least. But if the video is astonishingly good and is directly relevant to your child's application or college interest (such as to the filmmaking department for a major), have the teen call to find out if a video is in order.

Offbeat marketing gimmicks have no place in college applications. Kids, with or without parental prodding, sometimes come up with an inspiration they hope will help make their application stand out and influence its appeal. One student sent in pencils stamped with the words "Admit John Doe," using, of course, his real name. No one smiled in the admissions offices that got them. Discourage, even forbid, your student from such foolishness. As a Texas admissions consultant points out, "A student's grades, essay, and activities are what will get him in. Not the meaningless extras."

REMINDER *DOS* AND *DON'TS*

Do remember that colleges have their own reasons for admitting students. Some years they may need a particular balance—geographic, talents, extracurricular activities—that may or may not bode well for your child. "The better schools seek a class with some deliberateness, and there is no way for a parent or student to know what is going on," advises Dodge Johnson. "Some years a college may be short on debaters but long on theater majors—you can't have an idea what they may want in a given year." The result: Of two students with seemingly identical strengths, one with the "right" extracurricular interest that year gets in, the other does not.

Do remember that schools look for students who are good, solid achievers without any particular area of special talent. "In some cases high school leadership positions are nothing more than popularity contests," points out R. Russell Shunk, associate dean of admissions at Dickenson College. "Someone else gets the work done. That's the kid I want to talk to. He or she is going to be the solid contributor on the campus."

Don't compare your child to siblings, friends, or other kids you hear about. Keep in mind your child will be reviewed for his own set of strengths, and a college evaluation may be quite different from what you imagine.

Don't call the admissions offices without a legitimate excuse after applications are filed. Probably the only excuse in that category would be a significant change that might affect an admissions decision, such as your teen's winning a prestigious award or having her art displayed at a local museum. A letter *from your child*, with a request to have it attached to her application, may be the most effective way to handle noteworthy changes.

SAVVY PARENT TIPS

Admissions officers are pretty much in accord about the way they rank various parts of student applications. Here, in order of importance, are the areas of concern and how officers judge them.

Academic Record

In brief, the academic record offers admissions people three and one-half years of a student's life at a glance. Its value can't be overestimated: It can open—or close—the acceptance door.

Admissions officers look not only at the grades but also for trends in grades. Is there steady improvement? Can a glitch such as a poor year be explained by a family, health, or emotional problem? They also want to know if the student challenged himself; a B in English honors may earn him more points than an A in the regular curriculum. If an obviously bright student opted out of honors courses, they'll wonder why. If the high school is well known as a difficult one, admissions officers will keep that in mind.

For schools that use the "formula/scores" basis of acceptance, the teen's academic record is not important. Students applying to these schools are evaluated and accepted solely on SAT test scores. However, only a few state schools use this evaluation system; most want to know more than what a student can do on one day's test.

Testing Scores

The Scholastic Assessment Tests have raised the rancor of various academics and students for decades, but they remain one of the few ways to rank students on a national basis. They are, at least for the immediate future, here to stay.

SAT I tests a student's general knowledge and thinking ability. Divided into verbal and math sections, the two combine to carry a perfect score of 1600. Students typically take the test two or more times, and most schools accept the highest grade earned in each section. There are exceptions: The University of Michigan, for example, accepts both scores from the same testing session only; however, the student may decide which session to submit.

SAT II tests are known as the achievement tests and are given in specific areas, such as history, a foreign language, or chemistry. There is considerable latitude in whether a student needs to submit SAT II scores, and the student has the benefit of deciding *after* receiving the scores whether to submit them. Obviously, a student should take SAT IIs only in subjects in which he has done well and only if required by the colleges to which he is applying. Check individual college catalogs for up-to-date information.

Students have leeway about when to take the SAT II exams. As a rule, it's wise to take a subject test as quickly as possible after the student has completed studying the subject in school and the material is fresh. It's also a good idea to take most SAT IIs before senior year, when tensions are high because of everything else going on. One exception is the SAT II in English, since material learned during the first semester of senior year can help boost that SAT II grade.

The American College Testing (ACT) exams are similar to the SAT II achievement tests. These are required most often by some colleges in the Midwest, the West, and the South.

Not all schools require standardized tests as part of admission. Bates College and Franklin and Marshall are two examples of schools that do not. You can locate others in most college reference books, in individual college catalogs, or on the application forms themselves.

Extracurricular Activities

However frenzied your teen—and you—might have been running from activity to activity, this is the time to bless him for it. Schools want students who get involved and stay involved—sustained involvement is of primary importance. Specific types of activities are less important than their mere presence. Colleges look for any sincere interest, hobby, or avocation.

Even seemingly offbeat activities have impressed admissions officers. A student who writes movie reviews for the neighborhood paper; a dart player who takes part in official competitions; a national marble champion; a dancer who was part of Lincoln Center's annual "Nutcracker" troupe—all of these have been effective hooks for students hoping to achieve a distinctive profile. Some might seem irrelevent to parents, but how many marble champs apply to the same college in a given year? Be sure too that your child includes information about any handicap he's overcome or family circumstances that required him to take charge in an unusual way.

The Application

Applications should be both legible and neat. Even though you may have to search out a typewriter, do so, because admission officers prefer neatly typewritten forms unless the school accepts computer disk applications.

Due Dates

Missing a due date can mean being dropped from consideration. At the very least, being late is guaranteed *not* to impress admissions personnel. Be sure your student keeps his calendar marked with all pertinent dates and checks it regularly. Check with the testing agency and the high school to be certain scores and records are sent within the proscribed time; kids have been rejected because colleges didn't get their ACT or SAT scores or high school transcripts in time for their review.

Diversity

Diversity is a tricky situation for applicants because it has to do with the internal balance a college wants and so affects the student in ways she can't change. Part of the background mix colleges look for is socioeconomic; part is racial. Schools also hope to establish some geographical balance. If a university is looking to pull students from a certain area of the country and you happen to live there, it's your child's good fortune. There is a message in that which is simply to suggest your teen consider schools outside the area her fellow classmates are applying to. If this is the year her fellow seniors all want Stanford or Berkeley, for instance, she should broaden her list to include midwestern or eastern universities. The parameters of diversity are something to keep in mind when rejections and acceptances come in.

The Student's Interest in the School

If you take the time to look at the application process from the schools' point of view, you'll see how difficult it is for them. They want to be sure they fill the number of places they have in the upcoming class. Most don't have the luxury of long wait lists to cull from should they need to. Schools in this position, especially smaller ones, appreciate having a real sense of how interested applicants actually are. Will the student they want accept an acceptance? If your child's answer would be yes, she can strengthen her message in several ways. An enthusiastic personal interview is one way. "An interview," notes a midwestern admissions officer, "tells us the student took the time to find out what we're about." The message is enhanced if she sends in her application as quickly as possible. And, of course, the tone of the application and essay can send the message as well. If your child honestly wants a specific school, she shouldn't be shy about letting the school know it's number one in her book.

Chapter Six

HELP—AND HELP FOR HIRE
■■

Getting into college has spawned an industry of its own. With so much available, making the decision about who or what actually can help your child could become a monumental challenge. Should you use the school's guidance counselor or a private education consultant? If it has one, is the high school's SAT review course good enough, or do you need to go for a private SAT tutor? How will your child fare prepping for the SAT with computer software? If your child has learning problems, should you see yet another expert—can another one really help?

Added to your dilemma is the problem of Other Parents. "It seemed like every time I turned around there was yet another parent telling me I couldn't possibly *not* give my girl a particular review course or time with such-and-such consultant. I was a nervous wreck worrying Gale wouldn't get into the college she wanted and it would be my fault because I hadn't obtained this huge assortment of expensive help," says a mother in Hempstead, New York.

Your first inclination when considering help is no doubt your child's school. After all, education is its business, and who else would know better about different colleges? Well, yes and no. "I've seen three kids through the college-entry process," reports a father in Detroit. "Two of the counselors were wonderful. We didn't have to go any further than their office to get the information and support we needed throughout the whole time. But the third one! He was a disaster—not interested and, I suspect, not very knowledgeable."

Private schools often have excellent counselors. One reason: The list of fine schools their graduates attend is a marketing tool for attracting new students. That dollars-and-cents investment makes it worth their time to help their students get into top-ranked schools. The one problem you may find in private schools is that the counselors may pressure too much for top schools. While those names look good in the school's brochure, you'll want to be sure these are college choices your child really wants.

You can evaluate the counselor at your teen's school in several ways. First, discuss the matter with parents who worked with this person in years past. Their experiences and observations are apt to be dead on unless your child has an unusual and particular need, such as a school that caters to special interests. Then watch the counselor to see what the interactions with your child are like. You are looking in part to see what schools the counselor promotes for your student. They should match your teen's interests and abilities. Both public and private school counselors may fall into the trap of pushing the same schools over and over again. "I found my son's counselor usually took the path of least resistance.

He knew admissions officers at several schools and he pushed students in that direction," recalls a Houston mother. "Frankly, the schools weren't always appropriate."

Another quality you should be on the watch for is how the counselor handles students' self-esteem. Some high school counselors tell students they won't get into a college because they aren't in the top half of the class. "Parents should be on the lookout for this kind of thing and be prepared to support their child if it happens," warns independent education consultant Francine Block. "The students in the lower half have many schools available to them and hearing an unnecessary remark like that can be shattering," she adds.

"I wasn't the best student in the class, but I had pretty solid Bs," reports a student from the Washington, D.C., suburbs. "My counselor told me straight out that she thought I should apply only to junior colleges. I had my heart set on a four-year school, but I was so depressed by her appraisal of me, I almost didn't pursue it." This student's parents took note of what was going on and, through their encouragement, she applied and was accepted at an excellent, small, four-year school in Pennsylvania.

Other counselors can turn out to be your child's greatest source of support and hiring an independent consultant would be redundant. "My son's school counselor has been wonderful," enthuses a mother from Oregon. "Her office has been the place he's turned to throughout—he not only gets information squared away, he comes home feeling good about himself."

THE SCHOOL COUNSELOR CHECKLIST

Following are questions to help you determine how effective your student's counselor will be in helping to find the right college for her.

- Is he starting early enough? Winter of junior year is the most opportune time for students to begin working with the counselor, if not before.
- What is the counselor's background? Does he have experience in the field, or is he the hockey coach doing double duty?
- How many years has he been guiding students through the search process?
- Does he keep up to date by going to conferences, visiting campuses, and talking to admissions offices about changing policies and practices?
- Is he providing adequate information about schools so your child and you understand whether they might be good choices? He should be clear about size, locations, specializations, strength of departments, and the like.
- Does the counselor help your child understand himself and his needs better? Is he taking the time to steer him toward schools that will match his particular learning style, strengths, and interests?
- How many students is the counselor working with? Even the best one can be overwhelmed if hundreds of students are waiting at his door.
- What colleges and universities have students working with the counselor in previous years gone on to attend? Are there plenty of schools on the list that interest your child?

Sometimes an independent, albeit expensive, counselor is the best choice for everyone. "For us it was the only way to go," reports one father. "When our son first started working with the consultant, you could tell he felt freer, less constrained by the whole thing. Anytime I'd ask him about a deadline, he'd say, 'Ask the consultant—she'll fill you in if you need it. I don't want to.' As I saw it, the consultant could more dispassionately channel, focus, and pace the work that had to be done. I was relieved; it meant there wouldn't be any warfare on the homefront."

There are a number of reasons why your family also might benefit from an independent. The most obvious, of course, is that the school counselor isn't working out. This might be because he has too many students to work with, or due to a personality clash with your child. Consider, too, if it is a highly competitive high school, there may be many students applying to top schools—including yours. In that case you may want to have someone watching out just for your child, in part to be sure she has adequate backup choices.

Other reasons may relate to circumstances about your child. If any of the following describe yours, a private consultant route may be the way to go.

•Does your child have a learning difference, emotional disability, or physical difference? Today many consultants specialize in these areas and have a solid knowledge of student needs and opportunities, including which colleges really do have helpful resources and appropriate programs. Many colleges claim to have a handle on this pressing need, but not as many have programs that are truly beneficial. This person also can lead you to proper testing personnel and tutors if called for and can obtain the right to untimed SAT tests. Untimed tests can make the difference of 100 points or more for a child with a learning difference.

•Is your child balking about getting the college-search process going? Instead of having you be the bad guy here, fussing and fuming to get things under way, it might be easier—and more comfortable—to have an outsider become the facilitator.

•Does your child feel she needs more personalized attention? She may think she will do better with more one-on-one guidance, and if she feels that way, she probably will.

•Would your child benefit from advice and training about presenting herself more effectively? An independent consultant can step in and give help that would be harder to accept from a parent.

It's not just students who can benefit from the services of independent consultants. Parents have been known to appreciate them as well. These people are particularly helpful when the family is stuck with expectations and agendas that are causing confusion or hard feelings. Do you have your heart set on your alma mater or on a profession that you feel will be best for your child? Consultants can cut through potentially volatile situations like these with objectivity and help clear the air for everyone. They are there to work with you if you are part of the process—or to keep you at bay if you are the type who becomes overly entrenched.

Another advantage of private consultants is often the rapport they have with admissions offices. Since they may have more time than overscheduled school staffers, Pennsylvania consultant Francine Block points out, they sometimes have more time to visit colleges and opportunity to schmooze with the admissions staff. "I can make it clear in conversations that a problem which may crop up on a student's record had to do with special circumstances," says Block. Of course your child can relay this information in a personal statement or letter accompanying an application.

Parent caution: A consultant is paid in part to speak up for the student. One who is too aggressive is going to dampen most colleges' enthusiasm. Before you hire, consider the aggression level. And don't ask any private consultant, even a modest one, to write a recommendation for your child. Colleges are well aware that a consultant is paid by parents and is going to write about only a student's finest qualities.

SELECTING THE CONSULTANT

So you've decided a consultant is the way you want to go. Before you lift a phone, you should know that anyone can become a consultant—there are no screening, licensing, or controls whatsoever. This lack of regulation calls for particular investigation on your part before you hire.

The first order of business is to check that the consultant has a solid educational and/or counseling background. Ask about previous work history; many counselors have retired from school positions and have long been involved in the field. Membership in the Independent Educational Consultants Association is worth asking about, although some excellent consultants don't belong. A sterling recommendation from someone you trust is one of the best possible routes to a good consultant. When you first talk, be sure you understand exactly what her services will cover. Repeat back to her so that you know your concept is accurate.

It's wise to have a get-acquainted meeting before you commit. Come prepared with a list of questions to ask. (The questions in "The School Counselor Checklist" on page 80 will serve well in this instance too.) Allow your child some time alone with the consultant. However much you may like a particular person, if your child doesn't feel this is a good match, you'll need to keep looking.

Consultants charge anywhere from $500 to $3,000 or more, a flat fee that covers from the first meeting through the acceptance celebration. Should you need specific advice or guidance in one area only, a few consultants can be hired on an hourly basis.

GEARING UP FOR THE SATs

A lot of controversy surrounds prep courses for the SATs. Those who stand behind them, both parents and students, claim they give test-takers an edge. Says one mother: "The instructor made it an interesting night for my two boys. The review course became almost a game—the boys had such a good time taking trial tests, they preferred that to their homework." When it came time for the actual tests, this mother recalls that her sons were "less anxious. They knew what to expect and they were comfortable because there were no surprises."

Because so many students do take review courses, or even work with a private tutor, it's tough to say no to your child. "In this competitive environment, I don't see how parents can do anything but give the course to their kids," says one mother frankly. "When everyone else is doing it, you're going to put your child at a disadvantage if you don't."

Well, maybe. Not all kids need the review course. To help you decide if your child is among them, Richard Hresko, academic director of Q.E.D., an educational service company, suggests you have her take a sample test. You may obtain some in any number of review books on the market. Give it to your child on an untimed basis. "If the student gets everything more or less correct, all she needs is practice to get up to speed," Hresko explains. "You can do that for the student yourself."

On the other hand, if the SATs will address material your student has not covered, a review course is probably in order. You can provide instruction yourself, of course, but the success will depend heavily on your child's level of co-operation. A North Carolina mother found the vocabulary reviews were a lively part of the evening for her and her daughter. "We both enjoy words and we had a really good time together going over lists," she recalls. Her daughter's score went up a full 120 points after the mother-daughter review sessions. Other parents aren't as lucky and they end up coping with a great deal of teenage angst. "I took over working with my son to prepare for the math test," reports a Dallas father. "We worked for an hour every night, and there were times I had to physically drag him to the table. His score went up 100 points, but the weeks leading up to it were pretty horrible. In retrospect, I should have hired a tutor," says this dad.

Today a tutor is as close as your computer software store. Scout around among the offerings—new review programs appear on the market frequently. One may appeal to your child more than being obligated to a teacher—or you—for a given number of nights at a preordained time. In addition, software programs are inexpensive, an effective alternative to costly private courses.

The College Board's official guides and bulletins, available in the high school guidance office, contain much useful information on SAT I and SAT II services, registration, preparation, and test taking including dates and subject of achievement tests (SAT II) and scores.

You don't need to decide in the early stages whether your child will do better with services that go beyond the high school staff. Start with the school. If you hit a stumbling block, there still will be time to find the assistance you need. For instance, you may not know until a few months into the search that your child doesn't work well with his counselor. Or you may discover he needs some SAT reviewing after the first set of scores come in. There is plenty of help out there—waiting and willing—ready when your child needs it.

Chapter Seven

WHERE THE MONEY IS
■■■

Of the million or so students who start college each year, you can bet many of them are receiving financial aid of one sort or another. Fortunately, your student also has numerous potential sources of money—if you know where to look. Finances are an issue you should tackle early in the search for several reasons. Your success, to some degree, depends on being among the first in line. Having early estimates of your college financial obligations also will help determine to which schools your child may apply. You don't want to be in the heart-rending position of having to say no to a child who is set on a school because you discovered late in the game you couldn't fund it or find funding.

Financial aid comes in literally thousands of forms and just as many amounts. The existing options number in the hundreds of thousands, begining with college scholarships and substantial federal grants and ending with small esoteric money awards.

What follows is a basic look at the overall financial picture. It will guide you in how to determine if you are eligible for financial aid and provide the steps to take to capture those college assistance dollars. It's a complex and often burdensome procedure, with rules and regulations that change frequently, and what you'll read here is just the beginning. The keys to success, besides starting early, are to keep the search organized and orderly, and follow both the prescriptions and the schedule. Meeting deadlines and persistence should award you with success—and funds. Check financial applications carefully since each carries its own deadline.

SETTING THE COURSE

However deserving your child may be when it comes to brains and motivation, the reality is that much of the forty-two billion dollars plus in college financial aid available in this country is awarded on need, not merit. While families in the lower-income bracket are more likely to receive partial or full funding, make no assumptions. Even if you earn a substantial income, your family may qualify as a result of other financial obligations you have, such as two or more children in college at the same time, and, of course, the particular set of criteria of a given grant or loan.

To determine eligibility, you must fill out what is called the *Free Application for Federal Student Aid* (FAFSA—more on this follows) to determine what your expected family's contribution [EFC] will be. This has to do with a hard-and-set formula, not what you may think is a reasonable amount. You do this officially in your child's senior year, but you can get a workable estimate earlier with a practice federal financial form. The form can be found in some college advisory books, from the high school guidance office or from your state's department of higher education. Some software programs provide an electronic worksheet to lead you through the formulation on your home computer. (See Resources.) Once you've pinned down your expected contribution, you're in a better position to decide more specifically about what colleges you can afford.

THE FINANCIAL AID FORMULA

This is a precise procedure and the results carry a great deal of weight so approach filling out the financial aid papers with caution and care. Bureaucracy rules the world of government-related financial aid. Don't get yourself in a lather about the steps "they" require of you. Just do what they say and do it the way they want when they want. Pay particular attention to the definitions of key words that appear on forms before you fill them out. Even a tiny error can end up costing you in the long run, if not in money, in time.

You may obtain a Free Application for Federal Student Aid (FAFSA) form from the high school guidance office. Before you do the final one, get all the information correct on a practice form or photocopy. You will need your most recent tax forms, property value information, amount in savings, trust funds, and business value and liabilities if applicable.

Information from the FAFSA covering your family's income and assets, including your child's, goes into a government computer. The formula, determined by law, is applied and presto! your EFC becomes a fact of life for the year your child plans to start college. Within roughly four weeks after you file your "official" application, the U.S. Government mails you your *Student Aid Report* (SAR), which contains your expected family contribution. At this juncture, you may be asked to verify some of the information you submitted. The

Student Aid Report will be sent to all colleges you list. The colleges, not the federal or state government, finalize the financial package they ultimately offer the student.

You may as well learn the ropes the first time around—you'll be reapplying in the same manner every year. Your EFC can change substantially from year to year if you, for instance, have a second child moving into college or if one parent stops working to return to school and you carry not one but two tuitions.

Warning: The contribution included from your child's assets toward education is figured at a much higher rate than from your assets—a full 35 percent versus under 6 percent from yours. You also should give thought to ways you can structure your income during the year before your child starts college. For instance, if you'll be needing to cash in some investment money to finance college, do it before the end of the year that your child is a high school junior. This way it goes on your tax forms that year and not the crucial year she *starts* senior year, the year on which your first financial aid request is based. If you have a large professional fee or bonus due you, make similar a payment arrangement if you can.

Your EFC may come back saying, perhaps, $15,000. That's the amount the magic formula says you can afford to put toward your child's college costs. Should your child end up at a school that costs $15,000 a year, you'll foot the entire bill. But let's say she's hoping to go to a university with a $20,000 tab. In that case you are still responsible for $15,000, and you *may* receive the $5,000 balance in financial aid. Or you may receive just $2,000, in which case you'll have to take out a loan for the remaining $3,000 or find the money elsewhere, perhaps through scholarships from the private sector.

Once your official EFC comes out of the computer, it is sent off to all colleges to which your child is applying. Again, by doing the practice form first, you'll have a pretty good idea what the EFC—and your ability to pay—will be. You can save time and energy by not applying to schools that are beyond what you can possibly afford or, conversely, that you don't need as financially safe choices.

One important caveat: Some schools apply their own formula to the financial-aid information given on the FAFSA. Should the EFC come back higher than you had hoped, pursue the matter with the financial aid officers at the colleges of choice to see if their formula arrived at a different—and happier—conclusion.

FILLING OUT THE FORMS

Not to be a nag, but keep in mind that federal and state governments and colleges run out of money for scholarships and aid. Even so, eager beavers will have to contain themselves until January 1, the date after which you're allowed to mail in forms. That's because your income tax returns from the year before are a necessity. Be sure everything is ready to file your taxes ASAP so that you can follow up quickly with the FAFSA. It must be received no later than May 1, although you will, of course, have taken care of it many months earlier.

If your child is applying to a private college, it may require what is called the *Profile* as well as the FAFSA. Have your teen get the registration request form for the Profile immediately on starting senior year—timing is crucial for this. For information on which schools require the Profile, check the list printed on that request form and then double check with the catalog or financial aid brochure from each of the private schools in question. Also check their required filing deadline since these differ from school to school. Most are usually early, sometimes well before the end of the year. (You'll have to estimate your current year taxes.) You will then have to send the registration request forms to the College Scholarship Service in Princeton, N.J., which will send you the application form itself.

While the FAFSA is to determine the amount of public funds the college will put in your student's financial package, the Profile determines what, if any, he'll get from the school's private funds. It's a long and complicated form ("It asks everything but the amount of gold you have in your teeth," says one financial aid officer), but the results can make it well worth the effort.

Those looking for loan assistance available through state agencies will need the *Loan Application Promissory Note* available at most local lending institutions. States administer several federal loans (the Stafford and PLUS in particular) through a program with Guarantee Agencies. Check with the college financial aid office directly at each college for more information.

Your child's guidance counselor can be a huge help in sorting out who needs what and when. The picture is brightening, although slowly, in the area of financial complexity. One large northeastern university provides telephone access to financial aid possibilities for its accepted students. A parent or student punches in responses to six financial questions, and an estimated amount—pretty accurate for those with high or low incomes—can be faxed the same day or received in the mail a few days later.

* * *

This is the point at which the financial aid search gets interesting. Whatever the amount of your contribution, if your child is qualified and the school in question wants her, it may well make up the difference, even a substantial one, to assure her place in the school. The school may want her badly enough for a number of different reasons beyond her academic record: it could be a special diversity the college is seeking that year, an extracurricular interest, or other less obvious factor.

That's why you should never assume a particular school is out of reach. Financial aid from whatever source is meant to bridge the gap between what you can afford and what you need. And while it's true not every college can fund every needy student, it might fund yours. At Brandeis, a small private university in Massachusetts, over 55 percent of the freshman class receives financial aid. Most of it is need based, but the school also awards merit-based scholarships.

Don't go by what you hear about a school's policy last year. Stipulations, restrictions, and procedures change often and from year to year. The government may come up with a new tax break, a college may receive a huge endowment, new scholarships may surface one year that will never exist again.

You can get a pretty clear picture of which colleges provide substantial amounts of funding. Many guidebooks have a strong focus on financial matters. Look for one of these and start your money search by checking out which schools have money to give—and are giving it. You'll find out by examining the percent of students applying for aid, the percent receiving it, and the average amount of aid awards. However, this information will take you only so far in getting a financial focus since these matters change so often.

THE WIDE RANGE OF OPTIONS

The following list describes the general routes to financial aid. *Not all programs are closed to middle- and upper-income parents.* The headings are simplified, but you'll get a good idea of where the money is and what the programs are.

- •State and federal grants and college scholarships. State grants are reserved for state residents attending colleges in state and, for some states, out of state as well.
- •Loans including bank, government, colleges, and charities to parents or students.
- •Work/study awards in which the student is given a job, generally twenty hours a week or less, to pay off the awarded amount.
- •Private, corporate and organization grants, scholarships, and awards.

Scholarships and grants are categorized as gifts and do not have to be repaid. There's a faint distinction between federal and state grants (some private organizations also offer grants), generally awarded on need, and scholarships which are mostly awarded by colleges and private organizations. Scholarships are not necessarily awarded on need, but on academic achievement. Because of the fuzzy difference, the words frequently are used interchangeably. Loans, including work/study loans, must be paid back.

Here is an overview of some federal financial aid possibilities for those entering participating degree colleges or certificate (two-year) college programs.

• Pell grants range from $400 to over $2,300 based on need. You must reapply anually for renewal.
• Supplemental educational opportunity grants, from $100 to $4,000 according to need and the individual college's funding levels. These are renewable.
• College work/study awards are based on need and provide employment, either in the college or with a public or nonprofit agency. Earnings may not exceed the financial aid needed; hours can run from 15 to 40 per week (generally during vacations).
• Perkins loans can be as high as $20,000 for an undergraduate education. The average is $3,000 per year. This is a 5 percent interest loan, with payment to begin six to nine months after completion of school, and based on need. Students are often given ten years to repay the full loan.
• Stafford loans are available regardless of family need. Loan amounts vary according to the student's academic status and other financial aid. The student must already be enrolled at least half time in a two- or four-year program. Interest rates are set annually. For students who meet certain FAFSA criteria, the federal government pays the interest; otherwise the student may repay interest and principal after she has graduated.
• PLUS loans are also for students enrolled in two- or four-year programs. Parents may borrow regardless of income (but with an acceptable credit rating) and are limited to attendance costs minus other financial aid the student is receiving. Interest rates also are set annually.

Look within your state for various aid programs, especially designed for the state's colleges and universities and open to residents only. New Jersey, for example, has many, including: Educational Opportunity Fund Grants for students from educationally disadvantaged backgrounds (from the federal government; limited number available); the Edward J. Bloustein Distinguished Scholars Program for students based on scholastic achievement and class ranking without consideration of family income; and the Paul Douglas Teacher Scholarship Program for high school students who plan to become teachers. Undoubtedly your state has many programs as well. Contact the state department of education to get specifics.

YET MORE SCHOLARSHIPS

Estimates are that 300,000—yes, 300,000—scholarships and money awards exist for students seeking higher education. Your job is to find them. Many have been fed into databases and are also available in printed form.

Start looking for possible scholarships at your child's high school since the guidance counselor may well have access to a financial aid database and is commonly alerted to new aid programs and unusual sources of money. If not, check with a community college in your area and the colleges to which your child is applying. Some local libraries also have access to such a database. (See Resources.)

Rather than spend hours tracking one down, you have the option of hiring a professional to do it for you. Be sure to enlist a reputable service since this is a field full of people who make money preying on anxious parents—and give nothing or little in return. Ask for a reference from your child's guidance counselor or from friends who have been satisfied with the funding search services they hired.

Naturally you'll check with the colleges to which your child is applying. Many have substantial amounts of money for admitted students, although each has its own financial package arrangements. Ask for the printed literature concerning financial aid, which will give you a solid overview for each school of interest to your child. Check too if there are any scholarships around that may match your child's unusual talent or academic leaning. Keep in mind that small colleges sometimes have large endowments; hence, they can be generous with financial aid dollars. Many of the small, private colleges will give you an early aid estimate.

Go the the financial aid officer directly for this information. When you are visiting the campus, be sure your child has an appointment to meet with the financial director or officer to discuss the matter firsthand—and, if appropriate, stress his determination to attend this school.

Check other sources, such as your union or employer. Many large companies have programs that offer employees' children financial aid. While you're at it, check other large corporations in your area along with local organizations such as the Rotary, Lions or Elks clubs, religious groups, charities, and college alumni organizations, sorority and fraternity alumni chapters, some of which provide fairly substantial sums. Other groups to investigate are those for special interests, such as music or art, dance, and unusual sports. Additionally, associations for specific nationalities may have money for students. In many cases the funds might be only a few hundred dollars, but every bit helps. These plus a larger scholarship may be the bridge you need from your contribution to the total cost.

Don't get discouraged and don't give up. Every year

more educational funds go untapped because parents and students don't know they exist. Investigate any possibility that enters your mind as you go about the search. A phone call to a local group or association could be the means—a perhaps significant one—of bringing your college costs down to a reasonable amount.

NEGOTIATING A FINANCIAL AID PACKAGE

Often shocking to parents (in light of the time and work expended) is the fact that the financial aid package a college offers is not usually a no-strings-attached deal. Most packages have three not necessarily equal parts: (1) an outright grant from the government and/or a scholarship from the college; (2) a loan the student or parents will need to repay; and (3) a work/study award. You don't have to accept all parts of the package; to some extent, you can pick and choose.

Packages for the same student tend to contain similar components, but don't be surprised if you come across a great discrepancy in amounts. One student recently was offered a $3,500 package from one school and a $25,000 package from another. Go figure. This simply illustrates how complex, unpredictable, and unstandardized the financial aid system really is.

Be prepared to wait. Ideally you mailed your FAFSA and, if appropriate, your Profile, early in the game. Even if the financial office at the college has received your Student Aid Report from the government, it must wait until admissions decides to accept a candidate before it can begin to put a package together. It is possible that your child will be sitting quite a while, acceptance in hand, before the college's financial office figures out what its package will be.

You may get lucky and end up with a child who is accepted at two of his top-choice schools. Both are offering financial packages, the typical mixed bag of federal and state monies along with college or miscellaneous scholarships you have unearthed yourself. Assuming your child would like to go to either school, you are in an excellent bargaining position.

Discuss the situation with the high school guidance counselor, who will let you know how strong your position is. Then, assuming your child is a solid choice for both schools and will be happy in either place, try negotiating a little. Be assertive but not aggressive. Your child should inform both schools of the financial packages she has been offered. She must be completely honest about this. Financial officers talk to each other regularly, and they will uncover any embellishment. See if one or the other is willing to better the offer. It never hurts to ask.

THOSE IN THE KNOW

The effort it takes to keep your head clear as you go about tracking financial aid is marked. Best to locate one or two books that you find valuable and stick with them rather than read every book or pamphlet you can find on the subject. Attend sessions on financial aid sponsored by high schools or presented at college fairs. Finally, turn to those in the know who can help as you piece together the financial aid puzzle. These people include:

•Your child's school guidance office or counselor, or the special financial aid counselor if the high school has one.

•Financial aid directors at colleges to which your child is applying.
•The voices at the federal hot line for help in completing the FAFSA application and explaining the different loans and grants; call (800) 433-3243.
•Your state's Department of Higher Education.
•Financial planners who specialize in college financial assistance.
•Your accountant.
•Friends who have been through it.

As difficult, cumbersome, and time-consuming as the process of establishing financial aid can be, the rewards can be profound. A few thousand more dollars can make the difference between an education that will do and one that will serve for a lifetime.

Chapter Eight

CELEBRATION, SELECTION, AND SEPARATION

■■■■■■■■■■■■■■■■■■■■■■■■■■■■■■■■■■■■■■■

Finally, the colleges respond: from some, fat envelopes loaded with entrance and housing forms that herald the best possible news; from others, a negative. Although you can tell as well as your child which envelopes contain the good news and the bad, do not open any of them. These belong to your child; she did the work and it's her right to be the first to read them.

In the face of the intense competition for acceptance at certain colleges today, many of the brightest children or seemingly best qualified for particular colleges are turned down by the schools they prefer. By this point you will have prepared your child for the fact of not being accepted, but however much you have talked about this, don't be surprised by some intense reactions. Be sympathetic and don't harp on what he did wrong, even if he didn't prepare for the SATs. Remember, you signed on from the start to be his support team.

Your child may have had a long-cherished dream crushed, and you should respect his disappointment. It is probably the first major rejection he has had to cope with. As one counselor points out, being turned down by the college you had longed for is a much bigger deal than not making first string on the high school basketball team. Remind him that colleges look for students whom they feel will be the best possible match for their school. They may know better than your child if he would be happier elsewhere. Then too, there's the simple luck of the draw to consider. Schools with large applicant pools can't accept everyone, no matter how qualified some may be. And don't be hesitant to point out any college's downside, the aspects of it that your child wasn't happy about even as he applied for admission.

A few situations may merit having your child request the school reconsider her application. These include a significant increase in her grade point average since the fall, an athlete having made state playoffs or an all-state championship team, a student who has made an all-state chorus or orchestra, or any other accomplishment that is dramatic enough, say, to make the newspaper. The student should be the one to alert the school through a letter to the Director of Admissions. In the vast majority of situations, though, it's far better for both of you to switch your attention to the letters of acceptance.

TIME TO CHOOSE

For the past year or longer, your student has been discovering who he is and searching for a possible direction for his life, at least for the next several years. Your influence may have been such—as it is in many families—that one or more acceptance letters is from a college your child applied to in order to please or appease you. When the time comes to sort out acceptances, a clinical psychologist wisely reminds parents "to allow each child to grow in his own way, to develop his own sense of self, even if it's not what you had planned." Your goal throughout has been to make your child proud of *his* choice. Allow him to make it now.

Acceptance letters bring with them celebration and selection. Celebrating is the easy part, and do take advantage of it. After the months of worry and agony, your child deserves a fine dinner or other such treat to acknowledge both her work and its reward. Heap congratulations on each and every acceptance; the more opportunities you have to stroke your child's ego, the better. In addition, points out a long-time high school counselor, focusing on the positive instead of dwelling on the schools that didn't come through offers your child a much better balance and helps diminish any lingering feelings of rejection.

Selecting among schools may or may not be an issue in your home. Your child may be completely clear about the school he wants and acceptance is merely the beginning of his anticipated college experience. But many students, especially those who made careful application to schools that fit their personal college profile, might have to choose among several schools, any one of which would be that perfect fit.

If at all possible, visit or revisit the colleges your child is considering. An ideal situation is for your teen to spend a day or so there attending classes and socializing, perhaps with a friend who is already a member of the college's student body. As mentioned previously, teens have good instincts that often lead them to the right decisions rather quickly. By having a chance to hang around with students who would be college mates, your child might have all the information she needs. "Kids really do eventually find their own level," says a mother who has been through college selection twice.

Your child also could seek out any recent graduates he or the family knows or someone who graduated from his high school who is currently enrolled. A heart-to-heart about what a college is *really* like, from a student's vantage point, is invaluable. Other people who should be able to help your child focus the decision include the high school counselor or independent consultant if you worked with one.

Ultimately, if your child is not 100 percent behind her final choice, or if she harbors melancholy feelings about the school she didn't get in, you should remind her that selecting a college isn't making a marriage. Students can, and often do, switch from the school they started, some after the first semester, some after the first or second year. It is possible and feasible, and if the situation warrants a switch, the choice is there for the taking. Let her know you'll support and help her with that decision too.

PREPARING TO SEPARATE

In the next six or so months, you'll be preparing both your child and you for the inevitability of separation. It's time. It's appropriate. It's nerve-racking—for all concerned. Even though you both will weather the separation well and eventually probably be glad for it, there are some things you can do to make you feel better in the meantime.

First you should step in to help your child learn the life skills he'll need for living on his own. Be sure he knows how to do the following, or teach him if he doesn't:

•Money management, including how to handle a bank account, read a bank statement, and balance a checkbook; how to keep credit card spending under control and review bills; how to apportion money for living expenses.
•Time management—the essentials for allowing sufficient study time in relation to his course load.
•Laundry and ironing.
•Cooking basics and nutritional needs—the classic "freshman 15," that is, the fifteen pounds students typically gain in their first year, can be avoided.
•Car maintenance if appropriate.
•Personal safety measures, such as what to do when walking alone at night, taking note of being followed, and other street-smart tips.

The emotional separation may hang heavily over everyone. But remember, this is what all those years of child rearing were about. Having an eighteen-year-old ready to leave the family nest, strong and sure enough to go out into the world independently, is a testament to you. It means you've done your parenting job well. It doesn't mean your job as parent is over—it never really is—but the real work is behind you.

This is your child's show. You've been moving offstage for months, perhaps years, and it's time for your child to take over her own life. Prepare for some happy surprises. You may discover, as did Bill, a New York father of two, that the outcome can soar past your expectations.

"When my boy was in high school, he'd say he'd be happy if he could study what he wanted to study," recalls this dad. "I thought it was a cop-out and an excuse for his poor performance. We allowed him to 'own' his college search and to come to conclusions as he saw fit. I can tell you, he shocked us. In the college of his choice, he has become one of the most truly intellectual young men I know. He has enriched his life in so many ways. Whatever he chooses professionally, he has already turned himself into a very full person. A parent can't ask for more than that.''

RESOURCES

■■

This listing by no means exhausts the resource material for the college search. It is offered here to give you a starting place.

BACKGROUND ON COLLEGES AND UNIVERSITIES

Bookstores and libraries carry many more general books as well as many on very specialized topics.

- *The Insider's Guide to Colleges* (New York: St. Martin's Press)
- *Lovejoy's College Guide* (New York: Prentice-Hall)
- *The College Handbook* (New York: College Entrance Examination Board)
- *Peterson's Guide to College Admissions* (Princeton, NJ: Peterson Guides) New editions include an application planner on computer disk.

107

- *U.S. News & World Report: America's Best Colleges* (Annual magazine guide)
- *Money Magazine's Money Guide to Best College Buys* Annual. Note: Cover title changes.
- *Index of Majors and Graduate Degrees* (New York: College Entrance Examination Board)
- *Rugg's Recommendations on the Colleges* (Sarasota, FL: Rugg's Recommendations)
- *Colleges with Programs for Students with Learning Disabilities* (Princeton, NJ: Peterson's Guides)

ATHLETES' INFORMATION

- *Blue Book of College Athletics* An annual listing of colleges and the specifics about their sports programs including coaches' names and telephone numbers. About $30. Write Athletic Publishing, P.O. Box 931, Montgomery, AL 36101-0931, or call (205) 263-4436 to order.
- "NCAA Guide for the College Bound Student Athlete." Updated each year, the booklet offers information on eligibility, financial aid, recruiting, the different divisions and more. Single copies free by writing The National Collegiate Athletic Association, Publishing Dept., 6201 College Boulevard, Overland Park, KS 66211, or calling (913) 339-1900.
- *Peterson's Sports Scholarships and Athletic Programs* (Princeton, NJ: Peterson Guides)

MISCELLANEOUS

•*Independent Educational Consultants Association* (IECA) *Directory.* State-by-state member listing including the scope and focus of his/her practice: college admission, learning differences, summer placement, physically handicapped, and so forth. No charge. To order, write IECA, 4085 Chain Bridge Road, Suite 401, Fairfax, VA 22030 or call (800) 808-4322.

•"Facts About American Colleges." Updated annually, this quick reference booklet gives current and concise information by state and in chart form for over 1200 colleges and universities: area code and phone number, admissions person to contact, degrees offered, admission tests required, undergraduate enrollment, percent female and male students, tuition costs, average room and board costs, application due dates and more. Free from student's high school or at most college fairs, $4 from National Association of College Admission Counselors, 1631 Prince Street, Alexandria, VA 22314-2818 or call (703) 836-2222.

•"Students' Rights and Responsibilities." A two-page flyer that explains what is expected from colleges and universities in providing information and timely responses to applications. It discusses the student's responsibilities as well and provides details of wait lists, responding to admission decisions, and definitions of different types of admission conditions: early decision, early action, wait list, rolling and regular admission. To order, contact, National Association of College Admission Counselors, 1631 Prince Street, Alexandria, VA 22314-2818 or call (703) 836-2222.

ELECTRONIC SEARCH AIDS

Increasingly the search and application filing processes are being handled electronically—on disk or CD-ROM. More sophisticated programs are introduced as swiftly as the technology advances. You or your student will be alerted by high school guidance offices, peers, or advertising to new programs that simplify the job.

•*ExPan, Lovejoy's College Counselor, College View, College Link,* and *Apply*
Some of the programs available in high schools. Depending on software used, students can search electronically for schools matching their preferences, even see views of the campuses, produce letters requesting information, do an estimated FEC, and file applications with those colleges that accept computer-generated ones.

•*Introapp for Juniors*
An excellent way to begin the college search. For about $5, by filling in blanks on a computer disk and returning it, your child gives up to ten colleges of his choice a preview of his credentials, receives the schools' literature, and in many cases a personalized response. Can also be used early in the senior year. Introapp is often distributed in high schools. Or, to order, call (800) 394-0404.

•*The College adviser*
Recommends ten colleges that match the profile submitted on your child's form. He/she provides, among others, preference for setting, size, athletics, activities, career interest, possible areas of study, academic record . . . Student also receives descriptions of the colleges, costs, and important deadlines. Service costs about $40. From College Counsel,

209 West Central Street, Natick, MA 01760, or call (800) 248-5299.

• *College Finder* from *Money Magazine*

Students enter individual preferences, such as size, cost, and location, into the software program; a list of colleges meeting those requirements—ranked in order of importance of elements as specified by the student—appears on the screen. Also includes an electronic worksheet that helps determine financial aid eligibility. About $50. To order call, (800) 321-9479.

• *College Explorer*

About $125. With a database of some 2,800 colleges and universities, it provides information on everything from size and location to available financial aid and athletic programs. For DOS from the College Board; call (800) 323-7155. It's a slightly smaller version of their *ExPan* program, which is accessible to students in thousands of high schools.

FINANCIAL AID SOURCES (PRINT AND ELECTRONIC)

• *The Student Guide: Financial Aid from the U.S. Department of Education*—Grants, Loans, and Work-Study

Spells out the programs, procedures, basic eligibility parameters, provides state and national filing deadlines. Free from the Federal Student Aid Information Center, P.O. Box 84, Washington, D.C. 20044 or call (800) 433-3243.

•Financial Aid Need Estimator

A concise, easy-to-complete and confidential one-page form that American College Testing (ACT) processes for $5 and advises you of your estimated FEC and estimated eligibility for a federal Pell grant, plus attendance costs and admissions information (test scores, application deadlines ...) for three colleges your child selects. Contact: ACT at (319) 337-1040 or write American College Testing, P.O. Box 4029, Iowa City, IA 52243.

•*Cashe*

Distributed by National College Services Ltd. *Cashe* is a database of 2,000 institutions offering 200,000 public and private aid possibilities. Check the local high school (note: in Michigan, Illinois, and Indiana, among others, it is available to all high school students; community colleges in some areas service all county high school students) and the colleges to which your child is applying for free access and/or use charge, the average being under $15.

•National Scholarship Research Service

This service charges about $75 and has a database of over 200,000 private award sources. By indicating fields of interest, clubs, ethnic background, religious preference, parents' service history and affiliations among other criteria on the application, the company returns an extensive printout with possible private grant, loan, and scholarship sources including amounts, contact names, deadlines, and brief descriptions. For information call (707) 546-6777.

•*The Scholarship Book: The Complete Guide to Private-Sector Scholarships, Grants and Loans for Undergraduates* (Englewood Cliffs, NJ: Prentice-Hall)

Written by Daniel Cassidy of National Scholarship Research Service. This book has much of the information in their database although, depending on publication year, it may be missing the most current data. About $22 at bookstores, from NSRS, 2280 Airport Boulevard, Santa Rosa, CA 95403, or by calling (707) 546-6777.

• *College Costs and Financial Aid Handbook* (New York: College Entrance Examination Board)

COMPUTER ASSISTANCE IN FILING APPLICATIONS

As we become electronically proficient, more services become available to facilitate the application process. In addition to the software program used at your child's high school, she might investigate:

• *College Link*
Easy-to-use software allows students to apply to eight colleges (from a universe of 700+ including Harvard, Dartmouth, Duke, Stanford, University of Arizona, Lewis and Clark, and Oberlin) by filling out one application on computer disk. Each application is printed by College Link in the individual college's own format. A fee of about $35 includes mailing finished forms to the student for final attachments. There is no charge if a student's college application fees have been waived due to financial need. Call (800) 394-0404.

• *Common Application.* Students can apply to any of over 150 colleges by filling out one application in paper form or on disk. Common Application disks are free from student's high school or can be ordered for $10 from the National Association of Secondary School Principals, 1904 Association Drive, Reston, VA 22091. Call (800) 253-7746.

COLLEGE SEARCH TIME LINE MODEL

High school counselors begin working with their students at different times during the junior year or earlier. This time line model serves as a guide for parents who wish to track progress. Alter it according to your child's academic level, the types of schools to which your child is applying, and your family's schedule.

The simplest way to monitor deadlines, test dates, and periods planned for visiting is to enter them on a calendar reserved solely for the college search. Here are some of the more important goals and obligations for your college-bound child.

Junior year
•Review courses planned for the remainder of high school with counselor.
•Attend information sessions when college representatives visit the high school.
•Attend evening college counseling sessions with parents.
•Attend local college fairs and information sessions.
•Visit colleges whenever possible.

October: Take the combined PSAT/NMSQT, National Merit Scholarship Qualifying Test. (Purpose: to familiarize students with the format of SAT I to be taken later in the year and/or during the senior year and to become eligible for academic recognition and scholarship dollars from the National Merit Scholarship program and the National Achievement Scholarship Program for Outstanding Black Students)

114

December: Register for January SAT I and SAT II/ Achievements (optional).*

February: Register for March SAT I (optional).

March: Take SAT I (optional).

Register for May SAT I (optional).

Discuss registration and test dates for ACT and other SAT sessions student may need with guidance counselor.

Possibly visit a few colleges during a vacation (especially if the colleges are in session).

Begin to gather college catalogs and information about programs that might suit student's special interests or needs.

April: Register for June SAT I and Achievement/ SAT II (optional).

May: Take SAT I or ACT (optional).

Take (AP) Advanced Placement examinations (if applicable).

Study for June Achievement/SAT II (if applicable).

June: Take SAT I or Achievement/SAT II (optional but recommended for subjects in which study has been completed).

*Throughout, "optional" means if it applies to your child.

July/August: Continue to write for and gather college information.

Make a list of possible schools (request applications and literature only for ones seriously being considered).

Visit and be interviewed at as many of these college campuses as possible.

Begin discussing topics and concepts for an essay or personal statement.

Start collecting information about and sources for financial aid.

Senior year

September: Remind your child to meet with his guidance counselor regularly (if necessary).

Make tentative decisions with your child about how much will be spent annually on his education. Consider that you may be eligible for financial aid.

Ask your child to check for new scholarship sources; this information arrives regularly in high school guidance offices.

Help your child narrow down and finalize the list of schools to which he will apply.

Have him obtain missing information and applications and begin filling them out. Be sure he notes deadline dates for each on the calendar.

Plan for early decision and early action (optional)—enter application due dates on calendar.

Register for October ACT, November SAT I, and SAT II/Achievement Tests (optional).

Discuss who will write your child's recommendations.

October: Take SAT I (optional).

Register for the December SAT I or SAT II/Achievement Tests (optional).

Use any vacations throughout the fall to visit colleges on your child's list. Schedule interviews in advance.

Encourage your child to work on applications.

Have your child ask selected people to write recommendations and give them any necessary forms, envelopes, and return postcards. (See pages 68–69.)

November: Take SAT I and SAT II (optional).

File applications as they are completed.

Have SAT scores sent to "application" colleges.

Ask your high school to forward transcripts to colleges along with any other high school records or forms required by each college.

117

Begin financial aid applications. Forms are available in high school guidance office (optional).

Look into available private and public financial scholarship money.

December: Complete remaining applications and mail. Take SAT I and SAT II or ACT (optional).

First-semester grades count. Be sure your child studies and enters exam dates on the calendar.

January: File Federal Financial Aid Forms as close to January 1 as possible (optional).

Take SAT II (optional).

Check deadline dates for state aid forms and individual college aid forms, enter due dates and begin to complete forms (optional).

Explore other scholarship options.

Outstanding students may receive tentative acceptance.

February: Schools with rolling admissions and early notification dates may send their decisions.

Continue to look for scholarships.

March: Schools with rolling admissions and early notification dates may send their decisions.

April/May: Take AP (Advancement Placement) tests in May if applicable. Have your child make his selection from his college acceptances.

Have him notify college of his intention to attend by stipulated date; send in required deposit.

Have him alert all other colleges that sent an acceptance that he is going elsewhere. (This frees a spot in the freshman class for someone who may be on the wait list.)

June: **Graduation.**

APPENDIX

■■■■■■■■■■■■■■■■■■■■■■■■■■■■■■■■■■■■■■

After you have come to understand the college search procedure, and some of the complexities that determine which students a school accepts, take a few minutes to read through the following sample applications, based on the Common Application form used by many schools. (To order, see page 113.) The students—and their applications—are fictitious, but they are based on reality. Only one can be accepted; one can be wait-listed; and one must be denied a place. As you will see from reading the pertinent elements that have been supplied, each has strengths and weaknesses that would affect a school's choice, in this case, Charles University—also fictitious.

Keep in mind as you read through and "select" the successful candidates that universities look for balance in each incoming class. Academics are of supreme importance but so are the type of activities applicants pursue, whether they are leaders or teamworkers, the socioeconomic and racial mix and even the geographic. As you don the college admission officer's hat, you may more easily see how students who are clearly worthy may not find a place in some freshmen classes for a multitude of reasons.

CHARLES UNIVERSITY

Charles* is a highly regarded university of 8,000 students, with strengths in liberal arts, the sciences, and engineering. Founded in 1880 in a northeastern location, it is residential, coeducational, and highly selective. Although its environment is small town, it is two hours from a major city.

Personal and intellectual development of each student is sought through a core curriculum covering many areas, although there is considerable latitude in course selection. Competence in a foreign language is required for graduation. An attempt is made to admit as diverse a class as possible.

SAT scores must average at least 1,000 for candidates to be considered.

*fictional

122

CANDIDATE RATING FORM

Use this form to make your ratings of the candidates. Consider all the information available for each of the three sections (for example, in making an academic assessment, be sure to look at teacher comments and the essay, not just at the grades and scores), and make your notes and comments in the space provided.

	ACADEMIC (Grades, Recommendations, Test Scores, Essay)	EXTRACURRICULAR (Application, Recommendations)	PERSONAL QUALITIES (Application, Essay, Recommendations)
Kaneesha Taylor			
Jamie Jensen			
Jonathan Masters			

Albion • Alfred • Allegheny • American • Antioch • Babson • Bard • Barnard • Bates • Beaver • Beloit • Bennington • Bentley • Boston University • Bowdoin • Brandeis
Bryn Mawr • Bucknell • Butler • Carleton • Case Western Reserve • Centenary College • Centre • Claremont McKenna • Clark University • Coe • Colby • Colby-Sawyer • Colgate
Colorado College • Connecticut College • Cornell College • Dartmouth • Denison • University of Denver • DePauw • Dickinson • Drew • Duke • Earlham • Eckerd • Elizabethtown
Elmira • Emory • Eugene Lang • Fairfield • Fisk • Fordham • Franklin & Marshall • George Washington • Gettysburg • Goucher • Grinnell • Guilford • Gustavus Adolphus
Hamilton • Hampden-Sydney • Hampshire   Hanover • Hartwick • Harvard-Radcliffe • Haverford
Hendrix • Hobart & William Smith • Hofstra   Hollins • Holy Cross • Hood • Johns Hopkins
Juniata • Kalamazoo • Kenyon • Knox • Lafayette   **COMMON APPLICATION**   Lake Forest • Lawrence • Lehigh • Lewis & Clark
Linfield • Macalester • Manhattan • Manhattanville   Marquette • University of Miami • Middlebury • Mills
Millsaps • Moravian • Morehouse • Mount Holyoke   Muhlenberg • New York University • Oberlin
Occidental • Ohio Wesleyan • Pitzer • Pomona   University of Puget Sound • Randolph-Macon
Randolph Macon Woman's • University of Redlands • Reed College • Rensselaer Polytechnic • Rhodes • Rice • University of Richmond • Ripon • Rochester Institute of Technology
University of Rochester • Rollins • St. Benedict & St. John's • St. Lawrence • St. Olaf • Salem • Santa Clara • Sarah Lawrence • Scripps • Simmons • Skidmore
Smith • University of the South • Southern Methodist • Southwestern • Spelman • Stetson • Stonehill • Susquehanna • Swarthmore • Texas Christian • Trinity College
Trinity University • Tufts • Tulane • Tulsa • Union • Ursinus • Valparaiso • Vanderbilt • Vassar • Wabash • Wagner • Wake Forest • Washington College
Washington & Lee • Wellesley • Wells • Wesleyan • Western Maryland • Wheaton • Whitman • Whittier • Widener • Willamette • Williams • Wooster • Worcester Polytechnic

APPLICATION FOR UNDERGRADUATE ADMISSION

The colleges and universities listed above encourage the use of this application. No distinction will be made between it and the college's own form. The accompanying instructions tell you how to complete, copy, and file your application with any one or several of the colleges. Please type or print in black ink.

PERSONAL DATA

Legal name: __Taylor_____ __Kaneesha_____ __Eliza_____ _____ __F__
                 Last   *First*   *Middle (complete)*   *Jr., etc.*   *Sex*

Prefer to be called: __Kaneesha_____ (nickname) Former last name(s) if any: _____

Are you applying as a ☒ freshman or ☐ transfer student? For the term beginning: __freshman, entering 1997__

Permanent home address: __0000 West 136th Street_____
                                      Number and Street

__New York_____ _____ __NY__ __10000__
City or Town   *County*   *State* *Zip*

If different from the above, please give your mailing address for all admission correspondence:

Mailing address: _____
                              Number and Street

_____ Use until: _____
City or Town   *State*   *Zip*   *Date*

Telephone at mailing address: _____/_____ Permanent home telephone: __000__ / __000-0000__
                    Area Code   *Number*   *Area Code*   *Number*

Birthdate: __November 13, 1979__ ☒ Citizenship: U.S./dual U.S. citizen. If dual, specify other citizenship: _____

☐ U.S. Permanent Resident visa. Citizen of _____ ☐ Other citizenship. Please specify country: _____

If you are not a U.S. citizen and live in the United States, how long have you been in the country? _____

Possible area(s) of academic concentration/major: _____ or undecided ☒

Special college or division if applicable: __Arts School_____

Possible career or professional plans: __undecided career_____ or undecided ☐

Will you be a candidate for financial aid? ☒ Yes ☐ No If yes, the appropriate form(s) was/will be filed on: _____

The following items are **optional**: Social Security number, if any: _0_ _0_ _0_ . _0_ _?_ . _0_ _0_ _0_ _0_

Place of birth: __New York__ __NY__ _____ Marital status: __single 5'6" 140 lbs__
                   City   *State*   *Country*

First language, if other than English: _____ Language spoken at home: _____

If you wish to be identified with a particular ethnic group, please check the following:

☒ African American, Black   ☐ Mexican American, Chicano
☐ American Indian, Alaskan Native (tribal affiliation _____ enrolled ____) ☐ Native Hawaiian, Pacific Islander
☐ Asian American (country of family's origin _____) ☐ Puerto Rican
☐ Asia (Indian Subcontinent) (country _____) ☐ White or Caucasian
☐ Hispanic, Latino (country _____) ☐ Other (Specify_____)

124

EDUCATIONAL DATA

School you attend now __High School: Bronx Poly Prep_____ Date of entry _____

Address _____ ACT/CEEB code number _____
      City   _State_   _Zip Code_

Date of secondary graduation _____ Is your school public? _X___ private? _____ parochial? _____

College counselor: Name: __Monica Westman_____ Position: _____ _adviser_____

School telelephone: _____/_____ School FAX: _____/_____
            Area Code   _Number_   _Area Code_   _Number_

List all other secondary schools, including summer schools and programs you have attended beginning with ninth grade.

Name of School   Location (City, State, Zip)   Dates Attended

List all colleges at which you have taken courses for credit and list names of courses taken and grades earned on a separate sheet. Please have an official transcript sent from each institution as soon as possible.

Name of College   Location (City, State, Zip)   Degree Candidate?   Dates Attended

If not currently attending school, please check here: ☐ Describe in detail, on a separate sheet, your activities since last enrolled.

TEST INFORMATION. Be sure to note the tests required for each institution to which you are applying. The official scores from the appropriate testing agency must be submitted to each institution as soon as possible. Please list your test plans below.

SAT I (or SAT)	Dates Taken/ to be taken	Score	__596__	__501__		
			Verbal	_Math_	_Verbal_	_Math_
SAT II Subject Tests (or Achievements)	Dates Taken/ to be taken		_Subject_ _Score_	_Subject_ _Score_	_Subject_ _Score_	
ACT	Dates Taken/ to be taken		_English_ _Math_	_Reading_	_Science_	_Composite_
Test of English as a Foreign Language (TOEFL)	Date Taken/ to be taken	Score				

FAMILY

Mother's full name: __Eliza Taylor_____   Father's full name: __Charles Taylor_____

Is she living? _____   Is he living? _____

Home address if different from yours: Home address if different from yours:

Street: _____   Street: _____

City: _____ State: _____ Zip: _____   City: _____ State: _____ Zip: _____

Occupation: _school teacher_____   Occupation: _city employee_____
      (Describe briefly)   _(Describe briefly)_

Name of business or organization: _____   Name of business or organization: _____

College (if any): _graduated 1969, SUNY_   College (if any): _____ _no college_____

Degree: _____ Year: _____   Degree: _____ Year: _____

Professional or graduate school (if any): _____   Professional or graduate school (if any): _____

Degree: _____ Year: _____   Degree: _____ Year: _____

If not with both parents, with whom do you make your permanent home: _____

Please check if parents are ☐ separated ☐ divorced ☐ other _____

Please give names and ages of your brothers or sisters. If they have attended college, give the names of the institutions attended, degrees, and approximate dates: _only child_____

ACADEMIC HONORS

Briefly describe any scholastic distinctions or honors you have won beginning with ninth grade:

_____

_____

_____

_____

EXTRACURRICULAR, PERSONAL, AND VOLUNTEER ACTIVITIES (including summer)

Please list your principal extracurricular, community, and family activities and hobbies in the order of their interest to you. Include specific events and/or major accomplishments such as musical instrument played, varsity letters earned, etc. Please (✓) in the right column those activities you hope to pursue in college.

Activity	Grade level or post-secondary (p.s.) 9 10 11 12 PS	Approximate time spent — Hours per week	Weeks per year	Positions held, honors won, or letters earned	Do you plan to participate in college?
History Club	X X X	2 hours			will not
drama club	X X X	2-3 hrs			will
debate team	X X X	4 hours			will

WORK EXPERIENCE

List any job (including summer employment) you have held during the past three years.

Specific nature of work	Employer	Approximate dates of employment	Approximate no. of hours spent per week
stockgirl	neighborhood bookstore	(Jyear)	
CIT	local day camp	(F/S year)	

In the space provided below, briefly discuss which of these activities (extracurricular and personal activities or work experience) has had the most meaning for you, and why. Please attach an additional sheet if necessary.

_____

_____

_____

_____

_____

_____

PERSONAL STATEMENT

This personal statement helps us become acquainted with you as an individual in ways different from courses, grades, test scores, and other objective data. Please write an essay (250–500 words) on a topic of your choice or on one of the options listed below. You may attach your essay on separate sheets (same size, please).

1) Evaluate a significant experience or achievement that has special meaning to you.

2) Discuss some issue of personal, local, national, or international concern and its importance to you.

3) Indicate a person who has had a significant influence on you, and describe that influence.

Since I have just turned 17 as I write this, I would like to think that I am too young for tragedy to have entered my life. But it has and it has had a deep effect on me. Two summers ago when I was a CIT at our local day camp, one of the children was killed. It was the sort of terrible thing you read about in the newspaper and think, 'It could never happen to anyone I know.' But it did and it was one of the kids I was in charge of.

The details almost don't matter. We were walking into the baseball field when some teenage drug dealers were running after each other, firing their guns. Seven-year-old Quincy had the bad luck to be in the line of fire so instead of some kid who probably deserved the bullet in the back, our adorable boy got it. This was a scene so terrible and so sad I sometimes can't get it out of my mind.

It took me a long time to get over feeling depressed all the time. I decided that the only way I could deal with this tragedy was to learn something from it that would help me live a better life. I thought about this for many weeks and months trying to understand something good that might come from such a horrible thing. I spent a lot of time by myself, going for walks and writing in my diary, searching, searching, searching for some meaning.

What finally came to me wasn't a sudden answer I hoped for. I started to realize that I could never explain or understand why such a young life was cut down for no reason. That I have to leave to God because I don't get it at all.

127

But I could get something from it for me which is what I had set out to do. Most kids think they won't every really die. They figure that whatever they do--drive too fast, drink too much, do drugs or have unprotected sex--nothing can hurt them. I know that life can be very short and that what we do can hurt us, even kill us.

That is the negative part of what I learned. Fortunately I turned it into something positive for myself: the desire to live as best I can. It would be easy for me to take on a what-does-matter-anyway attitude, but I refuse to do that. Since I know that life can be cut short and at anytime, I have decided to make the most of everyday and every experience that I can. My parents haven't been able to give me some of the advantages that my friends have had, of travel and computers in our home, things like that. They have given me emotional strength. They are there for me always and I never doubt their love. This has made me strong and it helps me when I try for new things. I have become very active in school since my sophomore year. I knew I loved history and now I have been really exploring my African-American roots through the history club. I have always been sort of shy so I decided to join the drama club and the debate team to help me overcome that. I'm still shy but I'm learning the skills that make it possible for me to be more comfortable with others.

My college education has a great deal to do with my changed attitude toward life. Once I might have thought I could put off school or go to night school and that would be enough. If I am going to get the most from my life, I need a good education. This will help me get a first-rate job, but my need for education is more than the desire to do well professionally. I also need the exposure to great minds through the ages and the wisdom they offer me through the examples of their lives. College is where I will meet many of these people and I look forward to the experience. Of course, I also expect college to be fun and filled with many interesting and wonderful people whom I don't meet in books, but on campus!

Transcript

9th grade		12th grade first semester	
English	B	English/Lit	A
Spanish I	B	Political Sci	B+
Algebra I	A	Earth Science	B-
Biology	C	Advanced History	A+
Social Studies	A	Spanish IV	B+
Gym	B		
Computers	C		

SATs

verbal: 596

math: 501

10th grade	
English	A
Spanish II	B+
Geometry	C
Chemistry	B+
American Hist	A
Gym	B
Computer	B

11th grade	
English/Lit	A
Spanish III	B+
Algebra II	B
World Hist.	A+
Physics	C

EVALUATION

Please feel free to write whatever you think is important about this student, including a description of academic and personal characteristics. We are particularly interested in the candidate's intellectual promise, motivation, relative maturity, integrity, independence, originality, initiative, leadership potential, capacity for growth, special talents, and enthusiasm. We welcome information that will help us to differentiate this student from others.

Kaneesha is a very bright girl and really gifted in history and her perception of events and people. She has real insight and maturity that is unusual for a girl her age. She is an eager learner and a hard worker and I recommend her highly to your school.

--Miles Grohman, History Teacher

Please feel free to write whatever you think is important about this student, including a description of academic and personal characteristics. We are particularly interested in the candidate's intellectual promise, motivation, relative maturity, integrity, independence, originality, initiative, leadership potential, capacity for growth, special talents, and enthusiasm. We welcome information that will help us to differentiate this student from others.

Any school that Kaneesha elects to go to will be fortunate to have her. She is bright, hard-working and thoughtful beyond her years. My only concern for Kaneesha is that she is very close to her family and I think going away from home will be a difficult transition for her. But I don't see her giving up and even if it is hard at first, I think she will see her decision through to a successful conclusion.

--Monica Eastman, High School Counselor

EVALUATION

Please feel free to write whatever you think is important about this student, including a description of academic and personal characteristics. We are particularly interested in the candidate's intellectual promise, motivation, relative maturity, integrity, independence, originality, initiative, leadership potential, capacity for growth, special talents, and enthusiasm. We welcome information that will help us to differentiate this student from others.

Although Kaneesha has had some trouble with shyness, she has struggled to overcome it enough to add her presence to our team. Her presentation is still a little weak, but she has a fabulous understanding of the issues we debate. She has brought real dimension to the thinking of our team. I feel she will turn any expereince, including college, into a winning one.

--Stacey Weir, Debate Team Adviser

Albion • Alfred • Allegheny • American • Antioch • Babson • Bard • Barnard • Bates • Beaver • Beloit • Bennington • Bentley • Boston University • Bowdoin • Brandeis
Bryn Mawr • Bucknell • Butler • Carleton • Case Western Reserve • Centenary College • Centre • Claremont McKenna • Clark University • Coe • Colby • Colby-Sawyer • Colgate
Colorado College • Connecticut College • Cornell College • Dartmouth • Denison • University of Denver • DePauw • Dickinson • Drew • Duke • Earlham • Eckerd • Elizabethtown
Elmira • Emory • Eugene Lang • Fairfield • Fisk • Fordham • Franklin & Marshall • George Washington • Gettysburg • Goucher • Grinnell • Guilford • Gustavus Adolphus
Hamilton • Hampden-Sydney • Hampshire
Hendrix • Hobart & William Smith • Hofstra
Juniata • Kalamazoo • Kenyon • Knox • Lafayette
Linfield • Macalester • Manhattan • Manhattanville
Millsaps • Moravian • Morehouse • Mount Holyoke
Occidental • Ohio Wesleyan • Pitzer • Pomona

COMMON APPLICATION

Hanover • Hartwick • Harvard-Radcliffe • Haverford
Hollins • Holy Cross • Hood • Johns Hopkins
Lake Forest • Lawrence • Lehigh • Lewis & Clark
Marquette • University of Miami • Middlebury • Mills
Muhlenberg • New York University • Oberlin
University of Puget Sound • Randolph-Macon

Randolph Macon Woman's • University of Redlands • Reed College • Rensselaer Polytechnic • Rhodes • Rice • University of Richmond • Ripon • Rochester Institute of Technology
University of Rochester • Rollins • St. Benedict & St. John's • St. Lawrence • St. Olaf • Salem • Santa Clara • Sarah Lawrence • Scripps • Simmons • Skidmore
Smith • University of the South • Southern Methodist • Southwestern • Spelman • Stetson • Stonehill • Susquehanna • Swarthmore • Texas Christian • Trinity College
Trinity University • Tufts • Tulane • Tulsa • Union • Ursinus • Valparaiso • Vanderbilt • Vassar • Wabash • Wagner • Wake Forest • Washington College
Washington & Lee • Wellesley • Wells • Wesleyan • Western Maryland • Wheaton • Whitman • Whittier • Widener • Willamette • Williams • Wooster • Worcester Polytechnic

APPLICATION FOR UNDERGRADUATE ADMISSION

The colleges and universities listed above encourage the use of this application. No distinction will be made between it and the college's own form. The accompanying instructions tell you how to complete, copy, and file your application with any one or several of the colleges. Please type or print in black ink.

PERSONAL DATA

Legal name: Jensen   Jamie   Margaret
_____
            Last   First   Middle (complete)   Jr., etc.   Sex

Prefer to be called: _____ (nickname)   Former last name(s) if any: _____

Are you applying as a ☒ freshman or ☐ transfer student?   For the term beginning: __freshman, entering 1997__

Permanent home address: Rte. 00
_____
                                                  Number and Street

Alpine   ID   00001
_____
City or Town   County   State   Zip

If different from the above, please give your mailing address for all admission correspondence:

Mailing address: _____
                                                  Number and Street

_____ Use until: _____
City or Town   State   Zip   Date

Telephone at mailing address: _____/_____   Permanent home telephone: __000__ / __000-0000__
                              Area Code   Number   Area Code   Number
Birthdate: __August 30, 1979__   ☐ Citizenship: U.S./dual U.S. citizen. If dual, specify other citizenship: _____

☐ U.S. Permanent Resident visa. Citizen of _____.☐   Other citizenship. Please specify country: _____

If you are not a U.S. citizen and live in the United States, how long have you been in the country? _____

Possible area(s) of academic concentration/major: __Journalism, literature_____ or undecided ☐

Special college or division if applicable: _____

Possible career or professional plans: __journalism career_____ or undecided ☐

Will you be a candidate for financial aid? ☒ Yes ☐ No   If yes, the appropriate form(s) was/will be filed on: _____

The following items are optional: Social Security number, if any: _0_ _0_ _0_ - _0_ _0_ - _0_ _0_ _0_ _0_

Place of birth: __Alpine_____ __ID_____ _____   Marital status: _____
                City   State   Country

First language, if other than English: _____   Language spoken at home: _____

If you wish to be identified with a particular ethnic group, please check the following:

☐ African American, Black   ☐ Mexican American, Chicano
☐ American Indian, Alaskan Native (tribal affiliation _____ enrolled _____)   ☐ Native Hawaiian, Pacific Islander
☐ Asian American (country of family's origin _____)   ☐ Puerto Rican
☐ Asia (Indian Subcontinent) (country _____)   ☒ White or Caucasian
☐ Hispanic, Latino (country _____)   ☐ Other (Specify _____)

EDUCATIONAL DATA

School you attend now Alpine Valley High School _____ Date of entry _____

Address __Holmes Avenue, Alpine, ID__ _____ 00001 _____ ACT/CEEB code number _____

City   State   Zip Code

Date of secondary graduation _____ Is your school public? __X__ private? _____ parochial? _____

College counselor: Name: __Beth Johnson_____ Position: __advisor_____

School telelephone: _____/_____ School FAX: _____/_____

Area Code   Number   Area Code   Number

List all other secondary schools, including summer schools and programs you have attended beginning with ninth grade.

Name of School   Location (City, State, Zip)   Dates Attended

_____

_____

_____

List all colleges at which you have taken courses for credit and list names of courses taken and grades earned on a separate sheet. Please have an official transcript sent from each institution as soon as possible.

Name of College   Location (City, State, Zip)   Degree Candidate?   Dates Attended

_____

_____

If not currently attending school, please check here: ☐ Describe in detail, on a separate sheet, your activities since last enrolled.

TEST INFORMATION. Be sure to note the tests required for each institution to which you are applying. The official scores from the appropriate testing agency must be submitted to each institution as soon as possible. Please list your test plans below.

SAT I (or SAT)	Dates Taken/ to be taken	Score	563	532		
			Verbal	Math	Verbal	Math
SAT II Subject Tests (or Achievements)	Dates Taken/ to be taken					
			Subject	Score	Subject	Score	Subject	Score
ACT	Dates Taken/ to be taken					
			English	Math	Reading	Science	Composite
Test of English as a Foreign Language (TOEFL)	Date Taken/ to be taken	Score				

FAMILY

Mother's full name: __Helen Reese Jensen_____   Father's full name: __James Jensen_____

Is she living? _____   Is he living? _____

Home address if different from yours: Home address if different from yours:

Street: _____   Street: _____

City: _____ State: _____ Zip: _____   City: _____ State: _____ Zip: _____

Occupation: __parttime librarian_____   Occupation: __farmer_____

(Describe briefly)   (Describe briefly)

Name of business or organization: _____   Name of business or organization: _____

College (if any): __two years, Idaho Community Coll.__   College (if any): __no college__

Degree: _____ Year: _____   Degree: _____ Year: _____

Professional or graduate school (if any): _____   Professional or graduate school (if any): _____

Degree: _____ Year: _____   Degree: _____ Year: _____

If not with both parents, with whom do you make your permanent home: _____

Please check if parents are ☐ separated ☐ divorced ☐ other _____

Please give names and ages of your brothers or sisters. If they have attended college, give the names of the institutions attended, degrees, and approximate dates: __twin brothers, Chris and David, age 12.__ _____

ACADEMIC HONORS

Briefly describe any scholastic distinctions or honors you have won beginning with ninth grade:

EXTRACURRICULAR, PERSONAL, AND VOLUNTEER ACTIVITIES (including summer)

Please list your principal extracurricular, community, and family activities and hobbies in the order of their interest to you. Include specific events and/or major accomplishments such as musical instrument played, varsity letters earned, etc. Please (✓) in the right column those activities you hope to pursue in college.

Activity	Grade level or post-secondary (p.s.)					Approximate time spent		Positions held, honors won, or letters earned	Do you plan to participate in college?
	9	10	11	12	PS	Hours per week	Weeks per year		
Cheerleader		X	X	X		5			will not
Basketball team	X	X	X	X		5			will
track		X	X			3			will not
Prom chairman			X	X		2			will not
Senior Class Vice Pres.						2			will not
Managing Editor/High School Paper			X	X		3			will

WORK EXPERIENCE

List any job (including summer employment) you have held during the past three years.

Specific nature of work	Employer	Approximate dates of employment	Approximate no. of hours spent per week
Family farm		every summer	

In the space provided below, briefly discuss which of these activities (extracurricular and personal activities or work experience) has had the most meaning for you, and why. Please attach an additional sheet if necessary.

This personal statement helps us become acquainted with you as an individual in ways different from courses, grades, test scores, and other objective data. Please write an essay (250–500 words) on a topic of your choice or on one of the options listed below. You may attach your essay on separate sheets (same size, please).

1) Evaluate a significant experience or achievement that has special meaning to you.

2) Discuss some issue of personal, local, national, or international concern and its importance to you.

3) Indicate a person who has had a significant influence on you, and describe that influence.

Every thing changed for me when I signed up for my high school newspaper. I like everything about sports--watching them, taking part in them, cheering for them. I thought I might want to be on some kind of team as a professional even though I'm small. But then my girlfriend convinced me that I should try to do some work for the school paper.

I was surprised how much I love working on a paper. I love getting the news and finding out what the real story is. I love working on deadlines with the group, the way we have to push ourselves to be sure we make it. I love the way we work together and the fun we have as a team. This is definitely the field I want to be in for my life.

I haven't had the usual background for your school I would bet. Coming from a small western town has to be really different from most of the students at your school. But I chose your school because I wanted to be in the East and I want a chance to be around kids from a different world than mine. I really love Idaho and the mountains and the people here. But sometimes I think the environment and the people in my town are pretty limiting. They are so used to seeing things their own way and not realizing that other people can live happily in other ways. I want the excitement of a more challenging world and I am willing to work hard to get it.

Our school is better in Alpine than many in the area around us. Even though there are lots of farm kids who don't care very much about the issues that I do, they want

I understand that: (1) it is my responsibility to report any changes in my schedule to the colleges to which I am applying, and (2) *if I am an Early Action or Early Decision Candidate, that I must attach a letter with this application notifying that college of my intent.*

My signature below indicates that all information in my application is complete, factually correct, and honestly presented.

Signature _____ Date _____

to have a good education and the teachers have given us many extras. Last year we took a class trip to a Shakespeare Festival in Utah that was really great. I think maybe I got more out of it than some of the kids because that's exactly the kind of thing I want to have a lot of in my life. While many of the kids here see high school as the end of their formal education, I see it as a baby step. College is where I expect to take off!

Transcript

9th		11th	
English	B+	English/Lit	A
Algebra I	B	Algebra II	B
Social Studies	A	Physics	B
Biology	C	Spanish II	C
Gym	A	American History	A
Computer	A	Gym	A

10th		12th First semester	
English	A-	English/Lit	A
Geometry	B	Earth Science	A
Spanish	B+	Spanish III	B
Chemistry	B	Political Science	A
World History	A	Calculus	B
Gym	A		
Computer	B		

SAT's

verbal: 563

math: 532

EVALUATION

Please feel free to write whatever you think is important about this student, including a description of academic and personal characteristics. We are particularly interested in the candidate's intellectual promise, motivation, relative maturity, integrity, independence, originality, initiative, leadership potential, capacity for growth, special talents, and enthusiasm. We welcome information that will help us to differentiate this student from others.

Jamie is just fabulous! She has been truly wonderful on the newspaper, full of enthusiasm and she has a real insight into how to make a paper exciting and interesting. I feel she will be a big success at your school and in life and I recommend her highly.

--Jean Carlton, Newspaper Adviser

EVALUATION

Please feel free to write whatever you think is important about this student, including a description of academic and personal characteristics. We are particularly interested in the candidate's intellectual promise, motivation, relative maturity, integrity, independence, originality, initiative, leadership potential, capacity for growth, special talents, and enthusiasm. We welcome information that will help us to differentiate this student from others.

I have really enjoyed having Jamie in my classes. She is very responsive to the material we study and she has been eager about the extras I have built into the curriculum. She works hard for her grades, but she loves learning and she doesn't mind the work it takes to get a quality education. I am sorry to see her leave the west, but she seems to have her heart set on an eastern school and I support her desire.

--Chuck Swan, English Teacher

Please feel free to write whatever you think is important about this student, including a description of academic and personal characteristics. We are particularly interested in the candidate's intellectual promise, motivation, relative maturity, integrity, independence, originality, initiative, leadership potential, capacity for growth, special talents, and enthusiasm. We welcome information that will help us to differentiate this student from others.

Jamie is a most interesting student. She is a natural leader and extremely well-liked by her fellow students. She also works extremely hard at everything she does. I have only a few concerns about her matriculating in your college. Her family is a true western one and I think that she will have some adjustment problems in such a different environment. I'm confident that she will master that, but it will take her some time. Also, Jamie does have to work hard for her grades and she may be a bit at a disadvantage with the high school scholarship levels many members of your student body have. In spite of my reservations, I think she will succeed at your school and should have a place in the entering class.

--Beth Jolson, School Counselor

Albion • Alfred • Allegheny • American • Antioch • Babson • Bard • Barnard • Bates • Beaver • Beloit • Bennington • Bentley • Boston University • Bowdoin • Brandeis
Bryn Mawr • Bucknell • Butler • Carleton • Case Western Reserve • Centenary College • Centre • Claremont McKenna • Clark University • Coe • Colby • Colby-Sawyer • Colgate
Colorado College • Connecticut College • Cornell College • Dartmouth • Denison • University of Denver • DePauw • Dickinson • Drew • Duke • Earlham • Eckerd • Elizabethtown
Elmira • Emory • Eugene Lang • Fairfield • Fisk • Fordham • Franklin & Marshall • George Washington • Gettysburg • Goucher • Grinnell • Guilford • Gustavus Adolphus
Hamilton • Hampden-Sydney • Hampshire
Hendrix • Hobart & William Smith • Hofstra
Juniata • Kalamazoo • Kenyon • Knox • Lafayette
Linfield • Macalester • Manhattan • Manhattanville
Millsaps • Moravian • Morehouse • Mount Holyoke
Occidental • Ohio Wesleyan • Pitzer • Pomona

COMMON APPLICATION

Hanover • Hartwick • Harvard-Radcliffe • Haverford
Hollins • Holy Cross • Hood • Johns Hopkins
Lake Forest • Lawrence • Lehigh • Lewis & Clark
Marquette • University of Miami • Middlebury • Mills
Muhlenberg • New York University • Oberlin
University of Puget Sound • Randolph-Macon

Randolph Macon Woman's • University of Redlands • Reed College • Rensselaer Polytechnic • Rhodes • Rice • University of Richmond • Ripon • Rochester Institute of Technology
University of Rochester • Rollins • St. Benedict & St. John's • St. Lawrence • St. Olaf • Salem • Santa Clara • Sarah Lawrence • Scripps • Simmons • Skidmore
Smith • University of the South • Southern Methodist • Southwestern • Spelman • Stetson • Stonehill • Susquehanna • Swarthmore • Texas Christian • Trinity College
Trinity University • Tufts • Tulane • Tulsa • Union • Ursinus • Valparaiso • Vanderbilt • Vassar • Wabash • Wagner • Wake Forest • Washington College
Washington & Lee • Wellesley • Wells • Wesleyan • Western Maryland • Wheaton • Whitman • Whittier • Widener • Willamette • Williams • Wooster • Worcester Polytechnic

APPLICATION FOR UNDERGRADUATE ADMISSION

The colleges and universities listed above encourage the use of this application. No distinction will be made between it and the college's own form. The accompanying instructions tell you how to complete, copy, and file your application with any one or several of the colleges. Please type or print in black ink.

PERSONAL DATA

Legal name: Masters _____ Jonathan _____ Mark _____ M _____
           Last   *First*   *Middle (complete)*   *Jr., etc.*   *Sex*

Prefer to be called: Jon _____ (nickname)   Former last name(s) if any: _____

Are you applying as a [X] freshman or [ ] transfer student?   For the term beginning: _____

Permanent home address: 0000 Elm Street _____
                         Number and Street

Lakeshore _____ IL _____ 00003 _____
City or Town   *County*   *State*   *Zip*

If different from the above, please give your mailing address for all admission correspondence:

Mailing address: _____
                     Number and Street

_____ Use until: _____
City or Town   *State*   *Zip*   *Date*

Telephone at mailing address: _____ / _____   Permanent home telephone: 000 000-0000 _____
         Area Code   *Number*   *Area Code*   *Number*

Birthdate: May 30, 1979   [X] Citizenship: U.S./dual U.S. citizen. If dual, specify other citizenship: _____

[ ] U.S. Permanent Resident visa. Citizen of _____ . [ ] Other citizenship. Please specify country: _____

If you are not a U.S. citizen and live in the United States, how long have you been in the country? _____

Possible area(s) of academic concentration/major: physics _____ or undecided [ ]

Special college or division if applicable: _____

Possible career or professional plans: _____ or undecided [X]

Will you be a candidate for financial aid? [ ] Yes [X] No   If yes, the appropriate form(s) was/will be filed on: _____

The following items are optional: Social Security number, if any: 0 0 0 - 0 0 - 0 0 0

Place of birth: _____   Marital status: _____
           City   *State*   *Country*

First language, if other than English: _____   Language spoken at home: _____

If you wish to be identified with a particular ethnic group, please check the following:

[ ] African American, Black
[ ] American Indian, Alaskan Native (tribal affiliation _____ enrolled _____)
[ ] Asian American (country of family's origin _____)
[ ] Asia (Indian Subcontinent) (country _____)
[ ] Hispanic, Latino (country _____)

[ ] Mexican American, Chicano
[ ] Native Hawaiian, Pacific Islander
[ ] Puerto Rican
[X] White or Caucasian
[ ] Other (Specify _____)

137

EDUCATIONAL DATA

School you attend now __Lakeshore High school__ _____ Date of entry _____

Address __000 Shore Line Drive, Lakeshore, IL 00003__ ACT/CEEB code number _____

         City   *State*   *Zip Code*

Date of secondary graduation __June 2__ _____ Is your school public? __X__ private? _____ parochial? _____

College counselor: Name: __Kathleen Koonz__ _____ Position: __adviser__ _____

School telelephone: _____/_____   School FAX: _____/_____

        Area Code   *Number*   *Area Code*   *Number*

List all other secondary schools, including summer schools and programs you have attended beginning with ninth grade.

Name of School	Location (City, State, Zip)	Dates Attended

List all colleges at which you have taken courses for credit and list names of courses taken and grades earned on a separate sheet. Please have an official transcript sent from each institution as soon as possible.

Name of College	Location (City, State, Zip)	Degree Candidate?	Dates Attended

If not currently attending school, please check here: ☐ Describe in detail, on a separate sheet, your activities since last enrolled.

TEST INFORMATION.
Be sure to note the tests required for each institution to which you are applying. The official scores from the appropriate testing agency must be submitted to each institution as soon as possible. Please list your test plans below.

SAT I (or SAT)	Dates Taken/ to be taken	Score	728 *Verbal*	785 *Math*	*Verbal*	*Math*
SAT II Subject Tests (or Achievements)	Dates Taken/ to be taken	*Subject*	*Score*	*Subject*	*Score*	*Subject* *Score*
ACT	Dates Taken/ to be taken	*English*	*Math*	*Reading*	*Science*	*Composite*
Test of English as a Foreign Language (TOEFL)	Date Taken/ to be taken	Score _____				

FAMILY

Mother's full name: __Amy Louise Masters__   Father's full name: __Mark William Masters__

Is she living? _____   Is he living? _____

Home address if different from yours: Home address if different from yours:

Street: _____   Street: __000 Michigan Avenue__

City: _____ State: _____ Zip: _____   City: __Chicago__ State: __IL__ Zip: __00003__

Occupation: __executive director__   Occupation: __president__

   (Describe briefly)   *(Describe briefly)*

Name of business or organization:__Smith & Smith Public Rel.__   Name of business or organization: __International Carpets__

College (if any): __Northwestern University__   College (if any)__University of Chicago__

Degree: _____ Year: _____   Degree: _____ Year: _____

Professional or graduate school (if any): _____   Professional or graduate school (if any):__Wharton School of__

Degree: _____ Year: _____   Degree: _____ Year: _____

If not with both parents, with whom do you make your permanent home: _____

Please check if parents are ☐ separated ☐ divorced ☐ other _____

Please give names and ages of your brothers or sisters. If they have attended college, give the names of the institutions attended, degrees, and approximate dates: __siblings: none__

138

ACADEMIC HONORS

Briefly describe any scholastic distinctions or honors you have won beginning with ninth grade:

_____

_____

_____

_____

EXTRACURRICULAR, PERSONAL, AND VOLUNTEER ACTIVITIES (including summer)

Please list your principal extracurricular, community, and family activities and hobbies in the order of their interest to you. Include specific events and/or major accomplishments such as musical instrument played, varsity letters earned, etc. Please (✓) in the right column those activities you hope to pursue in college.

Activity	Grade level or post-secondary (p.s.) 9 10 11 12 PS	Approximate time spent Hours per week / Weeks per year	Positions held, honors won, or letters earned	Do you plan to participate in college?
Computer Club	X X X X	2 hours		no
Debating club	X X	4 hours		no

WORK EXPERIENCE

List any job (including summer employment) you have held during the past three years.

Specific nature of work	Employer	Approximate dates of employment	Approximate no. of hours spent per week
none			

In the space provided below, briefly discuss which of these activities (extracurricular and personal activities or work experience) has had the most meaning for you, and why. Please attach an additional sheet if necessary.

_____

_____

_____

_____

_____

PERSONAL STATEMENT

This personal statement helps us become acquainted with you as an individual in ways different from courses, grades, test scores, and other objective data. Please write an essay (250–500 words) on a topic of your choice or on one of the options listed below. You may attach your essay on separate sheets (same size, please).

1) Evaluate a significant experience or achievement that has special meaning to you.

2) Discuss some issue of personal, local, national, or international concern and its importance to you.

3) Indicate a person who has had a significant influence on you, and describe that influence.

I'm going to be pretty direct here. I have to go to college because it is the only way to a good job. I learn a great deal on my own, and I don't really think I need some of the ridiculous course work I know I will have to take to get my degree. But I also know the way the world works and that I have to play the game, at least while I am still this young.

The only thing that concerns me is using my brain as much as I can. The world is pretty rotten the way things are today and I don't see a lot of hope for most of the problems. I do think that there may be some answers through science and space that we aren't considering seriously enough now. I figure that with a good education in the sciences, I might be able to come up with some fresh answers. That will put me in the forefront professionally which I want. It should also earn me a lot of money which I would also like.

I find most parts of school really boring, and I don't hold a lot of hope that college will be too much different. I have to admit it will be sort of neat to work with professors who are the top of their field and can maybe teach me some stuff that I can't get from books. But we'll see.

I understand that: (1) it is my responsibility to report any changes in my schedule to the colleges to which I am applying, and (2) *if I am an Early Action or Early Decision Candidate, that I must attach a letter with this application notifying that college of my intent.*

My signature below indicates that all information in my application is complete, factually correct, and honestly presented.

Signature _____ Date _____

Transcript

9th grade		11th grade	
English	B	English/Lit	A
French	B	Algebra II	A+
Algebra I	A+	Physics	A+
Biology	A+	World History	B
Social Studies	A	French III	B
Gym	C	Gym	C
Computers	A+		
		12th grade first semester	
10th grade		English/Lit	A
English	A	Calculus	A+
French II	B	Advanced Physics	A+
Geometry	A+	Government	B
Chemistry	A+	Environmental Science	A+
American History	A-		
Gym	B-	SATs:	
Computers	A+	verbal 728	
		math 785	

141

EVALUATION

Please feel free to write whatever you think is important about this student, including a description of academic and personal characteristics. We are particularly interested in the candidate's intellectual promise, motivation, relative maturity, integrity, independence, originality, initiative, leadership potential, capacity for growth, special talents, and enthusiasm. We welcome information that will help us to differentiate this student from others.

I have had Jon in my classes for three years. His brain is astonishing, but he is a challenge for any teacher. He demands the most from you, but his attitude could definitely be better. In a word, Jon is arrogant. He is so much smarter than just about everyone around him that he has little patience for more ordinary people. Certainly I recommend him to your college, but I remind you that he will not be an easy student.

--Martin Shapiro, Science Teacher

EVALUATION

Please feel free to write whatever you think is important about this student, including a description of academic and personal characteristics. We are particularly interested in the candidate's intellectual promise, motivation, relative maturity, integrity, independence, originality, initiative, leadership potential, capacity for growth, special talents, and enthusiasm. We welcome information that will help us to differentiate this student from others.

What can I say about Jonathan? I have never had another student like him. Many of the kids today are well-versed in computers, but Jonathan has an uncanny and instinctive sense of the computer's workings and abilities. He could make the machine reach in ways that its creators may not even imagined! I can't think of a school that wouldn't be lucky to have Jonathan as a student although he can be wearing to be around. He is intellectually demanding--but that's good, right?

--Lucille Browne, Computer Teacher

Please feel free to write whatever you think is important about this student, including a description of academic and personal characteristics. We are particularly interested in the candidate's intellectual promise, motivation, relative maturity, integrity, independence, originality, initiative, leadership potential, capacity for growth, special talents, and enthusiasm. We welcome information that will help us to differentiate this student from others.

Jon is the most challenging student we have here at Lakeshore. Many of the teachers complain that he is too intellectually aggressive, and, yes, even arrogant. I feel strongly, however, that this reflects the fact that he finds the material being taught too easy to master. He absolutely should be at a fine university such as yours where he will have access to superior teaching and material. I suspect that any behavior negatives will disappear as he finds the satisfaction of an extraordinary learning environment. I strongly recommend him.

--Kathleen Koonz, Guidance Counselor

INDEX

■■■■■■■■■■■■■■■■■■■■■■■■■■■■■■■■■■■■■■